CONCILIUM

Religion in the Eighties

CONCILIUM

Concilium 139 (9/1980): Spirituality

CHRISTIAN OBEDIENCE

Edited by

Christian Duquoc

and

Casiano Floristán

English Language Editor
Marcus Lefébure

T. & T. CLARK LTD.
Edinburgh

THE SEABURY PRESS
New York

November 1980
T. & T. Clark Ltd., 36 George Street, Edinburgh EH2 2LQ
ISBN: 0 567 30019 6

The Seabury Press, 815 Second Avenue, New York, N.Y. 10017
ISBN: 0 8164 2281 8

Library of Congress Catalog Card No.: 80 50891

Printed in Scotland by William Blackwood & Sons Ltd., Edinburgh

Concilium: Monthly except July and August.
Subscriptions 1980: All countries (except U.S.A. and Canada) £23·00 postage and handling included; U.S.A. and Canada $54.00 postage and handling included. (Second class postage licence 541-530 at New York, N.Y.) Subscription distribution in U.S. by Expediters of the Printed Word Ltd., 527 Madison Avenue, Suite 1217, New York, N.Y. 10022.

CONTENTS

Part IV
Bulletin

Editorial

SINCE the Second Vatican Council hardly anything has been written which clearly and convincingly defends Christian obedience. What has appeared constitutes a series of detailed indications and suggestions which serve to restate correlations of obedience and liberty or obedience and authority. Since current opinion overwhelmingly favours liberty rather than authority, even within the Church itself the critical appraisal of obedience has been renewed and enriched. At the very least hardly anyone would dare assert that the most important virtue is obedience or that man was created to obey. The constitutive elements of this change of attitude are numerous and complex.

1. The first of these is an understanding and practice of religious obedience in the *traditionally absolute* sense which prevailed until the reign of John XXIII and the eve of the Council. Of course, towards the end of Pius XII's Pontificate the changes brought about by the war are already reflected in the treatment of Christian obedience in numerous publications by dogmatic, moral and ascetic theologians. These changes include the democratic increase in civil liberties, an increasing respect for public opinion, recognition of man's maturity, individual willingness to accept responsibility, a growing respect for freedom of conscience and the re-assessment of the dogmatic foundations of the virtue of obedience itself.

2. Another factor derives from the *political experience* of those European countries which replaced Fascist dictatorships by parliamentary democracies. Not all theological writings on obedience mention the emerging cultural milieu of secularised society. And some groups within the Church betray a certain reserve created by a fear that its religious members would water down the value and effectiveness of Christian obedience. Even today certain integrist groups which are secretly or openly anticonciliar betray the same fear. In the socialist states under Soviet influence and in those states which have military dictatorships founded on the so-called 'doctrine of national security' where there is direct confrontation between 'national liberation fronts' and the praetorian guards of these police states, the Church today is experiencing the tension between two different concepts of authority and liberty. This has a vital effect on the exercise and understanding of Christian obedience.

3. The third factor is *ecclesiological* and is an obvious element of the so-called 'first postconciliar era'. As an alternative to a hierarchical, sacral, bureaucratic and sacerdotal organisation, the setting in motion of a fundamentalist Church with a wide popular appeal, and which derives from an understanding of the People of God as organised into communities, creates new problems for Christian obedience. The principles on which preconciliar spirituality were founded, including a regard for Christian obedience coupled with respect for authority in the Church, were rejected. At times, this rejection was excessive and abandoned any attitudes of submission and resignation to authority. This period of confrontation with authority within the Church paralleled what was happening on political fronts towards the end of the seventies.

4. Today we are in the 'second postconciliar era' which dates from the last years of the Pontificate of Paul VI to these first years of John Paul II's reign. We live in a world whose institutions are unstable and where there is an ever-increasing problem of unemployment. In the face of military armament at all levels, there is a demand for disarmament as the only way towards peace. There is scandalous plenty and overwhelmingly obvious poverty. Society is undermined by insecurity and is in the

throes of an historical and political process of 'taking stock'. Many see the present pope as a symbol of moral authority and a powerful and charismatic leader who engages authoritatively in dialogue with the rulers of this world and who intends to unite the Church through the disciplined application of the dogmatic and moral principles of Vatican II without granting any concessions to the many postconciliar opinions which border on heresy. In this imposing and authoritative manner the intention seems to be the re-establishment of Christian obedience as a simple and absolute acceptance of the Church's authority.

5. However, a new theological and spiritual vitality is emerging from the Third World, and from Latin America in particular, which is making itself felt in the countries of the North Atlantic. It is based on the theology of liberation, sees the Church as a community and attempts a new valuation of popular Catholicism. Accordingly, the relationships between laity and priest, priest and bishop, missionary and native and the religious orders and the people reveal new possibilities for Christian obedience. There, the Church is not a monolithic structure which has been 'imported' nor is it a western Christian civilisation. Just as in other countries which are socially and culturally different from Europe, the Church wants to be and in fact already is the Church of the Lord which is faithful to the gospel and serves its people 'even unto death', and it is built on biblical, Christological and ecclesial foundations which have been renewed within the soundest traditions of the Church.

6. Like all the virtues, Christian obedience which has to be exercised today in a secularised socio-cultural context and in a pluralist Church divided by differing dogmatic, moral and ascetic tendencies looks for its roots in Christ *obediens usque ad mortem*. Using correct Christology as a basis, the virtue of obedience can be clearly and completely rediscovered. Of course, the obedience of Christ to the demands of the kingdom and the Father is paradigmatic and provides our example, but we cannot equal it. The virtue of obedience forms part of the faith and despite the demands imposed upon us by the faith, it is nevertheless necessary to emphasise various *facets* of this virtue so as not to reduce it to the mere acceptance of a totalitarian control. Let me indicate the main ones:

(*a*) Obedience is a *human act* made by a person as its creative author, who possesses personal autonomy, full knowledge, freedom and responsibility. To obey 'inhumanly' is not Christian.

(*b*) The believer obeys as *a member of the Church* within the Christian community. He is not the hierarchy's mere subject but a brother who shares the same faith, with a relationship of obedience towards those responsible for governing the Church and watching over the workings of the Spirit. It is paramount to have recourse to those brothers and sisters in the local community who are most open to the demands of the Spirit or whose knowledge makes them more competent. To isolate obedience from the ecclesial community is to curtail its Christian relevance.

(*c*) When Christian obedience is understood in terms of the *practice of the faith*, all believers—from first to last—are obedient to God, made known to us through Jesus the Christ who announces the Good News as he journeys towards the attainment of his kingdom and complete communion with the Father. Christian obedience is a 'common task' in which all believers have to take an active share, since all of them already possess the Holy Spirit, manifest through charisms and ministries in the Church. To reduce one part of the Church to silence through the imposition of absolute obedience is to deprive the Christian act of obedience of its very nature.

(*d*) *Ecclesial tension* is frequently created between established norms and the inspirations of the Spirit. At times, it is impossible to obey because authority is badly exercised or because it demands too much. It can also happen that no one obeys because no one is exercising authority. In every serious conflict between Christians, it is necessary to have recourse to competent colleagues and experts in their own fields, within the context of 'fraternal correction' which is genuinely based on the gospel and on humanity.

(e) Christian obedience is not merely a passive virtue exercised by subordinates towards those who govern. The objective of Christian obedience is not personal sanctification but the enriching of Christian life within society. Christian obedience is an *active virtue* because it requires the fidelity of all Christians to the demands of the Spirit of Jesus.

Translated by John Angus Macdonald

CASIANO FLORISTÁN

PART I

Displacements

Tullo Goffi

Deviations from Christian Obedience

ASCETIC WRITINGS have constantly reminded us of the duty of obedience. Can we hold that the meaning of this duty has never changed? No, it has had very different meanings and contexts. The uniformity was within the variable socio-cultural ecclesial context in which it operated. Although the word was the same, Christian spirituality has required different forms of obedience at different times. It was adapted to the values which were current at a given time. It has sought the most appropriate form of the virtue of obedience amid much disagreement.

Does the gospel message which includes obedience among Christ's saving teaching give this virtue a fixed meaning? On the contrary, there has been a progressive evolution in an attempt to reflect ever more closely the Lord Jesus's own loving obedience, according to the changing shape of the ecclesiastical community, the experience of the Christian people of the time and their dominant spiritual aspirations.

In spite of these changes in the form it took, obedience has always remained a Christian value trying to follow Christ. It would be wrong either to hold that obedience is not, properly speaking, a Christian virtue or that it should not be expressed in a changing historical human and Church development.

1. INEVITABLE VARIATIONS IN THE PRACTICE OF OBEDIENCE

The Christian community has the duty to live by the commandment of obedience in a manner appropriate to its own cultural period, always aiming to bear witness to it in accordance with the gospel's vision of love. Perhaps the Christian community has not always done this duty well.

Above all, the Christian community has sometimes shown a strenuous opposition to new cultural phenomena and held fast to the institutionalised forms of obedience as definitive. The Church establishment, which is necessary for telling the faithful what is appropriate in spiritual practice, does incline to privilege the ruling class. In order to maintain the existing order, the Church establishment presses the faithful to be united in the traditional custom of obedience to authority. It may forget that Christian obedience should also help this hierarchy to be converted to the meaning of the gospel as it applies at different times. Because it does not always do this, the hierarchical institution of the Church is liable to feel attacked when it encounters a more liberalised form of obedience. And thus the hierarchy when it stubbornly denounces any variation in the tradition of obedience becomes transformed into ideology and superstructure.

To what extent can opposition to an updating of the practice of obedience to suit the times be justified? The justification given is that the form of obedience already in existence and sanctified by the practice of the Christian community, whether rigorously deduced from an underlying social metaphysical system, or dictated by an invariable natural law, or founded on the gospel, can be declared as definitive and unchanging Christian behaviour.

In fact there has never existed a spirituality of obedience derived exclusively from a metaphysical system. The ontological meaning of a society has always been understood within a particular socio-ecclesiastical order. The spirituality of obedience has always expressed and been dependent on socio-cultural presuppositions belonging to a particular time.

The vocation to Christian obedience commands us to obedience which is not laid down in a final form (Luke 18:19; Matt. 19:17) but must follow the lead of the Spirit at any given time in the Church's history. A saint succeeds in being an outstanding example of obedience to the Christians of his time. Only Jesus Christ covers the whole perfection of obedience (Phil. 2:8). We become sharers in Christ's obedience within the bounds of the grace given in our own time (John 1:16). Usually the young perceive more readily and perhaps impatiently the precariousness of the traditional form of obedience.

A second source of deviation in the practice of obedience may arise from the fact that people follow new cultural forms of obedience without making the effort to convert and translate them into adequate evangelical expression (Matt. 20:20ff; Mark 10:35ff; Luke 22:24ff).

This happens whenever obedience is practised which depends solely on the demands of social subordination or of personal autonomy, without also expressing a vision of love in the Spirit of Christ.

The only thing that is mentioned is efficient social unity, the rights of authority, respect for personal dignity, the maturity or immaturity of subjects, discipline or democracy. Pius X who was concerned about the unity of the Church said: 'As for the multitude, it has no other duty but to let itself be led and to follow its shepherds like a docile flock.'[1] On the other hand St Augustine was tormented by the effort to express the evangelical meaning of obedience: 'We guard you because it is the duty of our office, but we also want to be guarded by you. We are your shepherds, but we too, like you, are sheep of the Shepherd. We are teachers for you, but like you we are under the Master, and disciples in his school.'[2]

2. THE ACTUAL EXPERIENCE THROUGH HISTORY

It is not possible here to trace the whole history of the various experiences of obedience throughout the history of the Christian community. We confine ourselves to a number of examples to show how obedience has been continuously adapted and given new ecclesiastical forms in a constant struggle to correct what went before.

Among the early anchorite monks government was reserved to the ancient fathers who had become 'pneumaticised'. The venerable ancient who directed the strict discipline appeared to be in total harmony with the Spirit; he possessed the charisma of the illuminating word. The novice strove to acquire from the 'pneumaticised' father the secret of becoming independent under the guidance of the Spirit.

Pachomius notes that such obedience could result in inconsistency and arbitrariness. As a corrective he proposed an 'obedience as a stable state so that the monk could live a life of continuous ascesis and live as a member of a monastic community'. The ideal of autonomy under the Spirit was integrated with the experience of *koinonia*.[3]

Was the proposal of a superior a way of ensuring a stable fraternal community or was it risking the possible arbitrary rule by one of one's fellows? To avert this risk, St Basil offered a written spiritual rule. It is not a rule in the sense of a canon, but a written collection of experiences according to the Spirit, experiences derived from the monastic centres of Egypt, Palestine, Syria and Mesopotamia. With this written guide the superior was enabled to examine and direct the monks as a spiritual father and not as a disciplinary officer.[4]

St Augustine noted that the community experience of these monks did not always display sufficiently clearly the communal dimension of the Church. Might not the monks who were closely bound together in friendship and free because in a state of grace, follow the Spirit without submitting to the authority of the Church?[5] Because the monks are not yet fully risen in Christ they can 'walk towards God in the footsteps of Christ (only) by obeying the precepts of the Church' (C. Marmion).

The introduction of the ecclesial dimension into the practice of obedience involved the danger of giving pre-eminence to the following of human regulations and not to listening to the Spirit. The need was felt to stress that obedience should be in the spirit of faith given that obeying the commands of the superior allows us to be 'led and ruled by divine providence' (St Ignatius Loyola).

Ecclesial obedience in the spirit of faith has in fact been practised according to a mode of totalitarian power. 'You must all pass through my head and my heart,' Mons. Escriva said repeatedly to spiritual directors.[6] This totalitarian style was also shown by means of the practice of prostrating the body which was sanctified by the liturgy itself. Submission is shown by the prostration of the body in which even the eyes are on the floor and the face hidden from view.

History shows a constant lessening of this bodily servility. In antiquity the subordinate prostrated himself on both knees before authority. In the middle ages he knelt with just one knee; in Shakespeare's time he merely bowed, bending his knees and leaning forward; in the seventeenth century it was just a bow. In the same way ecclesiastical custom gradually relented on *parrèsia*, that is freedom of speech in front of superiors, speech assured by the power of the Spirit. When Peter went to the house of Cornelius the centurion, the latter 'met him and fell down at his feet and worshipped him. But Peter lifted him up, saying, "Stand up; I too am a man"' (Acts 10:25-26).

Obedience in the spirit of faith has been described as an imitation of Jesus's obedience (John 8:29; Heb. 5:8; Phil. 2:8). Perhaps it has not been sufficiently noted that Christ's obedience has an aspect which we cannot imitate. Jesus was obedient through immediate contact with his Father, whereas our obedience must always be through the intermediary of a human person in authority. In the presence of God in Christ we must drop all our own autonomy (*suscipe universam meam libertatem*) so that 'we no longer live for ourselves but for him who died for our sake was raised' (2 Cor. 5:15). Obedience to God is identical with this faith. We should 'take every thought captive to obey Christ' (2 Cor. 10:5). But our obedience to God in Christ is through an earthly, ecclesiastical hierarchy. This cannot be a total abandonment of self even though it must always be an obedience in the spirit of faith 'in harmony with one another, in accord with Christ Jesus' (Rom. 15:5), because this is what creates love in the Church (1 Peter 1:22).

The socio-cultural context of today supports various claims to autonomy in the face of authority for the sake of the personal dignity of the subject.[7] In particular it affirms the duty to be responsible to ourselves in the very act of obedience. In what sense? St Thomas invites the subject to obey a command with responsibility and to 'act in this in accordance with one's own counsel as in other actions' (2a-2ae. Q. 104, 2 and 1). In the culture of today obedience is seen as a complement and development of the human person as a creator. The responsible autonomy of the subject must be integrated with the ruling wisdom of the superior. The holders of posts of responsibility in the community must not dictate personal laws, but harmonise the wise proposals made by members of the group.

It seems that this new form of democratic obedience has not yet attained sufficient experience of evangelical charity and brotherly Christian co-responsibility and that the superior has not yet assumed a proper charismatic function of spiritual father with the capacity to bear witness in the group to the unity of the mystical body.

This explains why in the decree *Perfectae caritatis* (n. 14) the mention of obedience appears to be insufficiently justified from the Christian point of view.

Although the new form of obedience has not yet acquired an adequate expression of evangelical charity, it is still strongly critical of the spiritual experience of the former manner of obedience. Among other things, it complains that the distribution of roles in the ecclesial community is not based upon the inclination or capacity of individuals, but on the principle of obedience. The personality of the subject and his vocation or talent does not count.

It is deplored that the exercise of authority is expressed in paternalism, relegating the faithful to the state of adolescence, especially women. Female convents are regarded as under the direction of the male ones (cc. 500, 3; 506. 2 CJC) and moreover they exist in subordinate social and ecclesial mansions.

When we try to give a more complete historical indication of the variations in the spiritual practice of obedience, we must admit that these variations were caused not only by the socio-cultural-ecclesial context but also by the particular character or spiritual vision of the people in authority or subject to them. Maybe these personal aspects were sometimes caused by human weakness but the Spirit uses them as an opportunity for personal sanctification. In this case we do not have total spiritual beauty but a human deviation redeemed by grace, not obedience as a genuine virtue but a carnal attitude converted into virtue through the spirit.

St Jeanne Françoise de Chantal (d. 1641) was aware of her noble birth and personal prestige in the convent of the Visitation, but spiritualised the affections she aroused in her nuns and demanded that their obedience should be in the spirit of filial charity, with a sense of sacrifice, patient humility, meekness and readiness to work.

Pierre Bérulle (d. 1629) was aware of his dignity as cardinal and presented obedience as one aspect of the hierarchical view of the universe. Divine graces come down into the soul, passing successively from God to Christ, to the Virgin, to the superior and finally to the subordinate. A prayer or a good action does not rise to God except by going up the same steps. Carlo Condren (d. 1641) who suffered from psychaesthenic depression, saw and lived by obedience as a form of self-annihilation: 'creatures do not have their own reality in themselves'.

From these examples we might remark that they are limited to obedience by religious. We should not forget that the spiritual experience of obedience is proposed as an ideal for all believers in the Christian community. Religious have the duty to show the faithful how the gospel should be lived in their day. When we see how the religious thought of and practised obedience at any given period, we see the ideal form in which it was proposed at the time for all believers.

3. OBEDIENCE, AN AMBIVALENT VIRTUE

Obedience is not only adaptable to the socio-cultural-ecclesial context of the period, but it contains certain contradictions in itself, it attempts to satisy opposing demands, and tries to reconcile antitheses.

Modern people for example feel they are in a dialectically contradictory situation when they submit to superiors. They look to authority as a charisma from whom they expect the curing of their spiritual ills, and at the same time see and condemn in this authority irrepressible power-seeking. Modern people are, on the one hand, increasingly subjected to powerful technical and scientific developments, and, on the other hand, they passionately desire total social autonomy. Never before have people been so dominated by extraneous forces and at the same time felt their humiliating subjection so deeply.

Authority and obedience, because they are ambiguous realities, often in the very act of making possible some good, attack other values. When authority is strong it has power and imposes order upon others, even when by doing so it may deny those under it the chance of giving spontaneous mutual help, the sense of personal responsibility and cheerful fellowship. An authority backed by an institution finds it easy to impose discipline upon the members of the community, gives a legal structure which overrides the behaviour of individuals, offers stability and security in moments of crisis. But this authority inclines to enclose even these crises within its own ideology, may become despotic and crush proposed innovations and suffocate attempts at autonomy.

How should the Christian obey in such a way as not to get stuck in the process of his own maturation, or be frozen within the immobility of the existing superstructures? He should join in organising socio-politico-ecclesial structures with responsible initiative and develop a methodical and constructive criticism of the dominant institutional forms. Thus the awareness arises of 'another power' with its own values beside the power of authority, and it is recognised that the greater common good does not exclude the absence of a certain conflict as a healthy force in the community.

All this requires that people should become increasingly better educated in wise participation in public affairs, that they have the will to revise systems which have historically proved to be closed in on themselves, authoritative and definitive, that they should be able to call upon and welcome the inner Spirit which makes each one of us the free child of God.[8]

The aspiration to personal autonomy is not confined to the matter of obedience towards orders from superiors. It is a restless aspiration which permeates the whole of society: an urgent need which may never be clearly fulfilled to feel free in every aspect of personal life.

Who now accepts conformity with fashion or convention in dress if they want to display their originality? In scientific research there is the problem of guaranteeing the personal dignity of the patient, the autonomous responsibility of the expert and the necessary democratic controls.

In politics there is the problem of the need to belong to a union or party in order to take part in public affairs and at the same time retaining one's own freedom of thought and action. And how should the media adapt to democratic controls if their influence is not to be despotic?

The ambivalence of obedience lies in the attempt to hold on to a completeness of values, since this is the cause of possible disagreement, in so far as desired values may be contradictory alternatives requiring one to be chosen at the expense of the other. Hence some have said that obedience is no longer a virtue. It would be more appropriate to hold that obedience, like everything else that is human, needs continual redemption from its innate ambivalence. St Paul reminds us that we are 'children of promise': the Spirit of Christ sets us free (Gal. 5:1).

4. SIGNIFICANCE OF DEVIATIONS IN OBEDIENCE

Are we of today striving for a practice of obedience that is more authentically Christian than that of yesterday? This is what is commonly believed because we are trying to discern the gospel's true message on obedience in a more conscious way.[9]

B

In fact the problem is not to formulate exegetically the gospel message on authority and obedience but how to translate it into the language of today, in a way that embraces all the values we prize and in accordance with our current socio-ecclesial problems. St Paul himself who was well aware of the utopian nature of the gospel message on the relations between men and women (Gal. 3:28; 1 Cor. 11:11f; 1 Thess. 5:19f), made particular proposals about the customs of his time which he said should be followed in a spirit of love (1 Cor. 11:3f; 1 Tim. 2:11ff). In the same way the Fathers accepted the gospel ideal but their particular proposals were to evangelise the customs of their time.[10]

We should not limit ourselves to preaching an abstract evangelical spirituality of obedience, but we must embody it in the actual custom of our time. We should do this even if it means expressing the gospel message of obedience in a partial, partisan and unilateral way.

Can we still respect a practice of obedience which makes an historical compromise with the gospel? Why undertake to be obedient if the Christian integrity of this virtue is impracticable? The Christian community is called to a holiness which develops during the history of salvation, which is measured by personal sharing in the becoming of the paschal mystery, which is always in need of conversion to come closer to the Lord. Only God is wholly good (Matt. 19:17).

At the same time evangelical goodness, including obedience is more a gift of the Spirit than our own work. Our daily awareness of our spiritual failings can help us become aware that true obedience is an ineffable grace which we must pray for to the Spirit. And this prayer is ever more effective the more we share in the paschal mystery of the Lord.

The Spirit helps us to translate the cultural form of obedience proper to our time into gospel terms and also enables us to see its relativity. The Spirit can help us today to quicken our desire for freedom and to show us that we are not prophetic enough in our witness to such freedom in Christ. He can help us to break through the socio-ecclesial bureaucratisation and also make us realise that we cannot rely on charismatic relationships alone. He can help us discern what is good and what is narrow or wrong among the modern forms of obedience and convince us that our spiritual journey must go on and on.

We should ask the Spirit to help us understand the providential nature of our spiritual restlessness, and teach us to discern the right form of the virtue of obedience for us and at the same time struggle to make this form more evangelical. We should ask him to make us obedient according to the style of our day but in a spirit of love, to make us obedient to the Church today as a grace which has the power to go beyond this form of obedience because it is a partial deviation. Every experience of virtue should be permeated by the consciousness of our own limitations and the aspiration to renew it through the gift of the Spirit.

5. AN OBEDIENCE BEYOND DEVIATIONS

In what way should we practise obedience to make us readier to be purified of its deviations by the Spirit? Revelation has given us some precious hints. The ancient prophets invited the chosen people to practise the law as an experience of the covenant with Yahweh. Jesus bore witness to a life of obedience which was a continual service of the heavenly Father's will (Matt. 7:21; John 4:34). St Paul invited us to 'be transformed by the renewal of your mind, that you may prove what is the will of God' (Rom. 12:2).

We must learn how to translate our every expression of obedience into service of the Lord. We must learn to transcend the mediation of human authority but accept in and through them the Spirit of Christ. Our every act of obedience should be a communication with God. Thus our obedience is guided by the gospel and bears witness to our own experience of love in the Spirit of Christ.

This does not mean that we should take every human command as the will of God. We are merely bearing witness that this precept is a way to go to the Lord, a way of coming into loving communion with God (1 Peter 2:18ff). We accept the command to express in and with it our love for the Lord. We are taking part in the dialogue with the Spirit which takes place within the history of salvation.

Such obedience proclaims the fundamental importance of the paschal mystery for our whole spiritual life. To the extent that we are risen in Christ it is possible for us to obey in communion with the Spirit. We are enabled to obey by sharing in the Lord's feelings. We are pleased to obey in the love of the Father. We are given the chance to overcome, at least partly, our inevitable failings in obedience. If we live by the paschal mystery, our obedience, even though it still expresses our own spiritual poverty, can become a manifestation of the spirit of the gospel in our time by the power of the Lord's Spirit.

Translated by Dinah Livingstone

Notes

1. Pius X, enc. *Vehementer nos* 11 February 1906.
2. St Augustine *Enarrationes in psal.* 126, 2-3; PL 37, 1969. See *Serm.* 23, 1-2; PL 38, 156.
3. See John Cassian *De Cenoborum institutis* 4, 1; 4, 30, 2; PL 49, 151ff.
4. See St Basil *Ep.* 223, 2; J. Gribomont RHE 54 (1959) pp. 115-124.
5. St Augustine *Vita communis,* Praeceptum VII, 1.
6. M. Angustias Moreno *El Opus Dei. Anexo a una historia* (Barcelona 1977) p. 61.
7. Aa. Vv. *La personalita autoritaria* (Milan 1973); As. Vv. *Figura e funzione dell'autorita nella communita religiosa* (Alba 1978); Aa. Vv. *Problèmes de l'autorité* (Paris 1962); T. Goffi *Di fronte all'autorita: evangelo ed esperienza umana* (Brescia 1974); M. Rossi *I giorni dell' onnipotenza* (Rome 1974); Card. K. Wojtyla 'Expérience de nos grands séminaires: l'obéissance et l'esprit de dépendance' *Seminarium* 21 (1969) p. 79ff.
8. St Thomas *Contra Gentes* IV, 22.
9. See L. McKenzie *Authority in the Church* (London 1966) p. 84.
10. See St John Crysostom PG 61, 289; PG 62, 543-545; St Ambrose CSEL 82, 238; 122ff; CSEL 32/1, 305, 16ff.

Edward Schillebeeckx

Secular Criticism of Christian Obedience and the Christian Reaction to that Criticism

IT IS always a valuable exercise to recall great traditions both in the religious and the non-religious spheres of collective human experience with the aim of creating a better and more human future for mankind. Such traditions may throw a critical light on certain blind spots when we consider them with our present-day, but nonetheless correct and new, attitude towards so many things and relationships. Provided that our vision is always critical, these early traditions can be both liberating and productive, thus making growth in man's true humanity possible.

Among these great human traditions, there have always been, on the one hand, 'pagan witnesses'. These were known as 'this world' in the Johannine writings and 'the people' in Mark. Present-day Christians usually call them 'the modern world'. They have always been critical of Christian obedience and of Christian humility, which is closely linked to this. It is always good for Christians to listen to this 'pagan' criticism, even when it is no longer completely correct from the historical point of view.

On the other hand, there are the 'Christian witnesses'. These are those whose experience of authentic Christian obedience has inspired them to criticise the secular self-sufficiency of man who does not appear to be aware of his loneliness and his non-solidarity.

I have been asked by the directors of the November issue of *Concilium* (on Spirituality) to provide, in broad outline, a survey of both sides of this mutual criticism. This would, of course, be quite a considerable historical task and to do justice to it would require a lengthy article. Here I can do no more than analyse a few fundamental phenomena drawn from history. These will be taken, on the one hand, from Graeco-Roman criticism of Christian obedience in antiquity and, on the other, from the resumption of that criticism in the modern world, within the new situation that has existed since the Enlightenment. This modern criticism has, after all, been to a great extent inspired by the Middle Stoa.

1. THE 'WORLD'S' CRITICISM OF CHRISTIAN OBEDIENCE
(a) The Greek Idea of Human Grandeur

Going back to a much longer Greek tradition, Aristotle expresses a supreme disdain for every form of servile subjection.[1] It should not be forgotten that this was, at that time, a social reality on a massive scale and that the élite owed its privileged position to slavery, something that was not necessarily borne in mind in the Greeks' theories of human grandeur. Man's grandeur was contrasted by that élite with servile subjection and this was expressed in the typically Greek view, which was later also taken over by the Romans, of man's 'greatness of soul' or magnanimity (*megalopsychia*; translated by Cicero as *magnanimitas*). This can also be rendered as great or fine humanity or, as we have rendered it here, as human grandeur. It was regarded by the Greeks as being based on an ethically good attitude to life (*kalokagathia*).

Although the basic attitude was seen as the same, the Greeks distinguished between two different aspects of this one human grandeur. On the one hand, there was the idea of an active and political grandeur, which characterised those who were manly enough to form grandiose plans and were able to carry them out. Such men were able to 'hold the world in contempt' if their cause was great enough and rise above it by their own human greatness and by the veneration of others. On the other hand, there was also contemplative and ethical grandeur, in which human greatness consisted basically of ethical excellence and of which Socrates was regarded by the Greeks as the prototype.[2] Because of his inner self-respect and self-image, this wise Greek man was able to transcend all the external vicissitudes of human life. What is more, this wise, contemplative man regarded the man who was politically great as a dangerous fool who had to be kept down. The external world could, it was thought, only be transcended by man's inner, ethical value.[3]

This ideal was given various forms in Greek philosophy. The Greek could, like Plato, scornfully transcend this shadowy world and look forward to the divine world of ideas as a model for the correct organisation of the terrestrial world-order that had been reduced to chaos by short-sighted politicians. On the other hand, he could also follow Aristotle and reject any order transcending this world, place God outside human life[4] and expect all salvation of and for men to come only from and through men and, what is more, only within life on this earth. The notion that it is better to give than to receive has a distinctively Greek background.[5] The ethical, active subject is dominantly virile and superior to whatever or whomever is the 'receptive subject', that is, the subordinate, dominated element or the 'female principle' of the receptive subject.[6] Because this magnanimous, typically male man has virtue in himself, he is able to transcend the terrestrial world outside himself, even in default of the latter, because he knows that he has, on the basis of his own inner virtue, a right both to be honoured by all other men and to all terrestrial goods. The Aristotelian man of grandeur keeps to the golden mean between vanity or boastfulness and 'smallness of soul' or pusillanimity (*mikropsychia* or *pusillanimitas*; sometimes called *humilitas* or modesty). Both these attitudes are vices, because they imply a mistaken knowledge of oneself, except in the case of the really small man, for whom such humility is suitable. The man who, however, has a sense of grandeur does what is good, not because it is offered by someone else, even a god, but because he regards this as good and beautiful in itself.[7] Such a man is 'autarkic'. He can do without everyone and everything and has no need of anything, not even God. In contrast with small and servile men, he will, laughing scornfully and condescendingly, ironically conceal his own grandeur[8] and he knows in particular that he is superior to those who have political power in this world and that he is above all superior in ethical widsom. His only need is for friends of like mind and he is satisfied with intercourse with them.[9] He is autonomous and free and at the service of the one great cause, regarding his own external life as nothing.[10] This humanly great man would normally be the king of the country.[11] He is conscious that he should have that status, but he is able, autarkically, to renounce the honour that others apparently begrudge him. This, then, is a brief summary of Aristotle's teaching.

Greek thought about this question, however, went even further than this. The Stoics were even more radical than the radically minded Aristotle, at the same time adapting his ideas so that they were more accommodating to men's religious needs. They denied, for example, the Aristotelian principle that man had some need of external goods before his acquisition of virtue. From the very beginning, it was sufficient for the wise Stoic simply to have a subjective ethical intention, on the basis of which he condemned not so much the outside world of sense-perception, as that world in so far as it lay outside man's free will and appeared as fate in contrast with man's freedom. The harmony of the world-order, that is, the will of God, could call on man to sacrifice his own individual aspirations, with the result that he would have to defer, as far as his own will was concerned, to the law of the universal divine Logos, which was Reason in all things.

Stoic condemnation of the world, then, is purely ethical. In contrast to Platonic and Aristotelian human grandeur, the greatness of the wise Stoic was accessible to all men—both the slave (Epictetus) and the emperor (Marcus Aurelius). This was the period of Graeco-Roman cosmopolitanism, the so-called brotherhood of all men: 'Homo, res sacra homini' (Seneca).

Unlike the original Stoics, the Middle Stoa, a little later, was aware of the illusory and utopian nature of man's direct knowledge of the will of God. Perfect harmony between human reason and universal divine reason was seen as a chimera. The new element that these Middle Stoics introduced into wisdom was that there had to be intermediaries between God's will and human will. In this way, we are able to know the will of God, at least with a probable knowledge, and carry it out, through the private natural tendencies of the individual things by means of which universal order is achieved. By obeying our private and individual natural aspirations, we translate the universal law in a probable and correct way. In other words, we obey God in this way. This Stoic view became extremely important historically in the whole of the western world, both Christian and non-Christian.

In this version of Greek philosophy, the dominant norm of human grandeur is man's subjection to the will of God. Despite this, however, this Greek attitude towards life (an attitude that was also adopted by the Romans, since this Greek ideal was universally disseminated by Rome in the later 'imperial' Stoa) was characterised by an exclusive trust in man's powers in his attempt to obey God's will. For the man of grandeur, praying to God was only a prayer of thanksgiving and never a prayer of petition or a supplication for help. (See Cleanthes' famous hymn to Zeus.) The Greeks did not, in other words, kneel in front of God and implore him for help. To do that would have been contrary to man's dignity and autarky. Seneca's saying: Deo parere, libertas est,[12] that is, man's freedom consists in obeying God, expresses a Stoic conviction that man owes his existence to God, but that, precisely for this reason, he no longer has any need of God and is able only to rely on his own powers.[13] According to this pantheistic view, trust in God is only possible in the mode of human trust in oneself. The climax of the 'pagan spirituality' of Greece and Rome was reached perhaps in the teachings of Marcus Aurelius, in which it is possible to detect signs of what Christians would call a humble obedience in faith. An example of this is the saying: 'Why should God not help us even in those matters that are within our power?'[14] Here, as elsewhere, this great humanist shows that he has some need of God, but at the same time even this humble confession is an expression of the Stoic's self-sufficient autonomy. We can therefore say that, in default of a correct concept of God and his creation, those qualities known as Christian obedience or humility could not thrive in 'pagan' soil. At the same time, however, the pride with which the Greek was human is also a criticism of Christian humility.

This Greek spirit (which was elaborated in various ways, including neo-Platonism later) came about as the result of a tragic experience of life. Looking at himself and his own human powers, the Greek could be optimistic and he was able to cope with life. He was, however, pessimistic when he looked outside, that is, at the 'world' or at society, believing that man was smashed to pieces by the vicissitudes of blind fate. Man's inner dignity and happiness could only be disturbed by things outside him. Salvation or human redemption had to be sought in some technique by which man was able to transcend the world on the basis of his own unthreatened and self-sufficient grandeur. Freedom, then, was, for the Stoics, a privatised and inner independence and it could in fact be accompanied by an absence of social and political freedom. But, even though they were religious, these philosophers never sought refuge with a god or implored him to send them a favourable fate. His own autonomous conscience bore witness to the fact that the magnanimous man did not, as a 'good man', deserve adversity and that, in adversity, not he, but fate was wrong. This *contemptus mundi* or scorn of the world was therefore the other side of the coin of man's autarkical grandeur and had nothing at all to do with a *contemptus sui* or a denial of oneself.

As soon as this Graeco-Roman attitude came in contact with the humble obedience of Christianity, it found itself in conflict with it. The Greek saw Christian obedience as a direct attack against man's grandeur.

(b) 'Pagan' Human Grandeur as a Criticism of Christian Obedience and the Reaction of Christians

(i) Christian Humility as Servile Cowardice

Pagan philosophers only condemned the Christian witness of martyrdom, an action described by the *Acta Martyrum* as the most powerful that a Christian could perform. Why, then, was this rejected by pagan philosophers, when the pagan *magnanimus* or man of great soul was ready to lay down his life for a great cause? It is, moreover, a historical fact that many Stoic philosophers were martyrs and either murdered or at least banished from Italy because of their ideals, which included criticism of society. Despite this, however, it is undeniable that high-minded pagan thinkers such as Epictetus, Marcus Aurelius and Celsus[15] regarded the obedience of Christian martyrdom as weak and cowardly pusillanimity and even as a perverse disgust for human life. They certainly did not think of it as human grandeur or *magnanimitas*. Their criticism of Christians was that they crept up to a god to implore him tearfully to help them and, in martyrdom especially, did not trust in their own autonomous powers.

(ii) Humility as the Only True Human Grandeur

The Fathers of the Church almost always began their arguments by making a distinction between genuine humility and its many spurious forms—after all, they were also Greeks! After this, they tended to respond to the pagan arguments with counter-arguments, insisting that only humility was true human greatness. In so doing, they frequently provided an analysis of the pagan attitude towards this concept. It is also remarkable that, with the exception of Augustine, both the Greek and the Latin Fathers accepted as their point of departure that the pagans also had a clear notion of humility. (This conviction persisted until the middle ages.)

Christians were aware, on the other hand, that the pagan author Celsus had said, in his anti-Christian polemic,[16] that Christian humility was a plagiarism taken from the writings of Plato and that, in doing that, the Christians had misinterpreted Plato. The Platonic *tapeinos* or humble man always bore witness to a 'well regulated' form of humility and, according to Celsus, that reasonable order was not present in Christian humility.[17] Christians, after all, permitted thieves and prostitutes to enter what they called the kingdom of God[18] and this was abhorrent even for the permissive Greeks.

Augustine, however, was firmly convinced that humility was an original Christian quality that was unknown among the pagans, who were in fact completely unaware of it.[19] The Greek Christian Origen dealt most fully with Celsus' criticisms. He too pointed to various possible caricatures of Christian humility.[20] He believed that authentic humility was a virtue that was practised only by great Christians, just as magnanimity was the privilege of great pagans. In other words, according to Origen, only saints were humble and only that form of humility could be called really human grandeur. Humility did not confront man with the world—it confronted him with God and the only suitable attitude for man in that situation was one of humble obedience. To humiliate oneself, then, was a patristic virtue which meant seeing oneself in relationship to God, who was, Origen taught, alone great, while every man, confronted with him, was small.[20]

Augustine expressed this patristic conviction very clearly: *Tu homo, cognosce quia homo es. Tota humilitas tua, ut cognoscas te.*[21] In other words, true humility consists in knowing that you are man, because true humanity is firstly being God's creature and secondly being bruised by sin. Knowing oneself in the light of God therefore brings about a humble obedience in faith and, by means of a radical change of the pagan concept, this obedience is called magnanimity or human grandeur.

Over and against pagan humanism, then, the Fathers of the Church stressed God's greatness and human misery. The patristic and, later, the medieval theologians (up to the time of Thomas Aquinas) were therefore able to identify authentic humility with magnanimity, thus mystically transforming the pagan concept. In patristic theology, the emphasis was on the grandeur of God who had mercy on man in his smallness. This emphasis led to a radical change in the typically pagan concept of the *contemptus mundi* or scorn of the world. In pagan philosophy, *spernere (despicere) mundum* or looking down on the world was the other side of the coin of man's autarkical self-assertion over the fortunes and misfortunes of fate that came upon man from outside. Scorn of the world was, in other words, an expression of human grandeur. On the basis of Christian faith in God's creation, however, this Greek *contemptus mundi* or scorn of the *world* was extended in patristic teaching to a *contemptus sui* or denial of *oneself*. *Spernere mundum* or looking down on the *world* became *spernere seipsum* or despising *oneself*. In other words, Christians regarded the human grandeur of the pagans confronted with the cosmic and social outside world as nothing, especially in the presence of God. In this way, a real confrontation with pagan thought was avoided and a purely Christian solution was found for the problem. There was, however, no question of a synthesis between pagan grandeur and Christian humility. A legitimate pagan criticism was not elaborated in a Christian sense. It was simply refuted. The relationship between man's liberation of himself and salvation in God's name was not solved, although this was the real pagan contribution that Greek philosophy could make to Christianity as a criticism.

(iii) Human Grandeur from God

Christians became more conscious of this problem in the twelfth century, although the non-religious version of pagan philosophy (that is, Aristotle's view of human grandeur) was unknown at the time. The ideas that were in fact known then were in the main those of the Middle Stoa. In the Augustinian tradition of the middle ages, Bernard made a distinction that remained predominant throughout the whole period. Briefly summarised, it is this: man can be seen from two different points of view. In the first place, he can be seen in himself, that is, in what he is in himself and would be without God, in which case he is nothing, mere dirt and shadow. He was, after all, created 'from nothing'. In the second place, he can be seen in his relationship to God the creator, through whom he is positively what he is and to whom he owes all his human greatness. His human greatness is therefore God's greatness in him.[22] Even a Stoic philosopher would probably say something of the same kind, although his spirituality would still be fundamentally different from the Christian's here.

This is very clearly revealed in Bernard's more precise definition of this distinction (which was strenuously opposed by Thomas Aquinas). According to Bernard, our human share in our humanity is sin and evil, injustice and disaster, whereas God's share in our humanity is goodness and salvation, justice and happiness.[23] The negative element is therefore our contribution, whereas the positive is God's, with the result that 'humility' points to man's contribution and magnanimity to God's. It would never, of course, have been possible for a Greek to express himself in this way! Even Bernard, however, was to some extent reserved in his belittlement of man, making a distinction between *humiliatio*, which is a humiliation forced on man from outside, and *humilitas*, which is spontaneously and happily accepted in a personal manner. In his own words, *humilitas iustificat, non humiliatio*,[24] that is, man is justified not by being humiliated from outside, but by a humility that he has chosen himself. Finally, we can only be humiliated by ourselves—a conviction which really reveals something of the attitude of the Middle Stoa. *Humiliari*, keeping oneself lowly, therefore has nothing to do, either in patristic teaching or in the Christian middle ages, with *se humiliare*, humiliating oneself. It is clear, then, that Bernard regarded the humble man as authentically autarkic and autonomous and, what is more, *causa sui*. Although his teaching is obviously in the patristic tradition, it also reveals something of the Greek idea of autonomy.[25]

We may therefore conclude by saying that pagan humanism stressed human grandeur as coming from and through man himself, even though, in the imperial Stoic tradition, it is also a gift from God. At the same time, this grandeur is entirely lacking in humility. Human grandeur is also accompanied, in this Graeco-Roman teaching, by an ignorance of God's true divinity. The Church Fathers and the medieval theologians, on the other hand, recognised the true grandeur of God, but failed to understand man's secular grandeur and to give it a proper place in creation. This failure coloured and frequently discoloured the concept of Christian obedience. It is therefore possible to say that both the pagan philosophers and the Christian theologians of that period failed to combine human grandeur with humility and, in the teaching of both, one of the two aspects was undervalued. This meant that each side failed to criticise the other legitimately.

(iv) Thomas Aquinas' Synthesis

An attempt to form a synthesis was made by Thomas Aquinas in the thirteenth century, when Christians came into contact with pagan and fundamentally Aristotelian conception of human grandeur. The fierce discussions that arose between 1250 and 1277 were the direct result of the shock that this contact gave to medieval Christians. Several theologians, notably Albert the Great, had prepared the way for Thomas's work of synthesis by pointing out the particular direction in which he should proceed. The fact remains, however, that it was Thomas alone who, after a long period of hesitation, formulated that synthesis into which the pagan criticism of Christian humility and obedience was assimilated and in which the pagan view was at the same time criticised. It cannot be denied that Thomas to some extent explains Aristotle's ideas away and christianises him in his synthesis, but, despite this, he displays a fine sense for his distinctively pagan impulse and in the long run does justice to this.

After some hesitation, then, Thomas made this synthesis, which is to be found especially in his *Summa Theologiae* 2a-2ae. Qq. 161 and 129. It dates back to 1271. He does not deny that the Church Fathers mystically transformed the pagan idea of magnanimity, but, on the contrary, admits for the first time that it was in many ways a right idea and thus criticises the traditional Christian view of man as a miserable creature on whom God has mercy.[26]

In Thomas's opinion, humility has nothing to do with the outside world or with man's fellow-men. It is only concerned with man's relationship with God. Whereas the Aristotelian virtue of magnanimity regulates man's passion for grandeur (as a mean between recklessness and despair) in the service of man himself and therefore also in the service of man's humanity, Christian humility regulates that same human passion in relation to God. Humility is therefore an essentially religious virtue. In the light of his faith in God's creation from nothing, Thomas is able to repeat the traditional distinction that man, seen purely from the point of view of man himself, has nothing of his own (that is, in contrast with God; all that man has of himself is sin), but that, seen in his relationship to God, everything that is positively present in him is a pure gift from God.[27]

This statement is, however, only apparently the same as Bernard had said in the previous century. Thomas, after all, makes an addition (which is fundamentally Greek), namely that man has a value of his own which is not exclusively derived from God: 'an inalienable human value that is peculiar to him'.[28] In other words, according to Thomas, man has a grandeur of his own and that grandeur cannot be made to vanish by a form of medieval mysticism. Man is a subject, even with regard to God, and is therefore responsible both for his good actions and for his evil deeds. No one else, not even God, is responsible for that man's actions.[29] He is magnanimous and is therefore able to know his own strength. He knows the extent of his capabilities and is not afraid to accept his grandeur. But, because he is also humble, he knows that his power is a gift from God. This knowledge does not, however, impede his human movement. It is clear, then, that Thomas was not concerned with the drama of God's grandeur as contrasted with the smallness of man, but rather with the drama within man himself, that is, the tension in man between human grandeur and human misery. Magnanimity is a virtue of human hope and is expressed through man's own power. It is also directed towards increasing man's humanity.

In this way, Thomas succeeds in rehabilitating man's trust in himself, which is a quality that is in no sense in opposition to the humility that presupposes man's magnanimity and at the same time includes it in faith in God the creator who brings salvation. 'Pagan' humanistic trust in oneself is therefore included in God's grace, which on the one hand heals bruised man and, on the other, enables him to share in community with God. Thomas is therefore clearly opposed to the patristic and medieval belittlement of man and restores his human trust in himself, stressing that his grandeur comes from himself and his own powers, although those powers are a gift from God and man often damages them. Christian hope, then, is included within the one perspective of salvation, which transcends all human power and to which man can only react with hope, and at the same time also includes man's human trust in himself *sub Deo*.[30] Only the man who obeys God absolutely in faith and expects all salvation to come from him alone is able to trust in his own strength to save that part of humanity in man and society that is both confirmed and transcended by God.

Thomas therefore provided the foundations for our own distinctively modern mode of life, which is not based on the monastic model of the middle ages, but has developed in accordance with more autonomous, profane structures. Despite the fact that, at the level of mysticism, he often makes pronouncements that are almost identical with those made by the Church Fathers and the medieval theologians, he cannot be regarded as working within the Augustinian tradition of the middle ages. Even at this mystical level, however, it is possible to distinguish a substructure in which man's autonomous human value is emphasised. Towards the end of the thirteenth century, the distinctively profane structures of the 'modern' world were beginning to develop[31] and the foundations for a non-monastic, Christian spirituality had been laid by Thomas. His restoration of humanism at the individual level in the sphere of Christian spirituality became the basis of his doctrine of social justice at the level of society.

The drama of the modern era that followed the period in which Thomas Aquinas was active took two forms. On the one hand, a few years after Thomas's death, Siger of Brabant's theory, which gave a very one-sided emphasis to pagan magnanimity, thus upsetting the balance in Thomas's synthesis, was condemned by the Church, mainly on the ground that Siger refused to call humility a virtue. On the other, there was, much later, in the sixteenth and seventeenth centuries (despite the emergence of neo-Stoicism), a strong tendency on the part of Christian spirituality to revert to an earlier Augustinianism, with the result that it became ineffectual in the modern world. By that time, Thomas's statement, emphasising both the Christian and the humanistic dimensions: 'A minimisation of the perfection of God's creatures is a minimisation of the perfection of God's creative power',[32] had been totally forgotten, with the result that the modern world looked outside Christianity for the man that it really needed.

As we have seen, Thomas laid the foundations for a structure which would have given form, within Christian obedience in faith, to man's pathos for large-scale undertakings to promote human development. He also provided the foundations for a complete trust in man as well as in his scientific and technical skill in solving the problems of the world. Despite this, however, it cannot be disputed that this human pathos, as first expressed in synthesis by Thomas, has become effective, for the most part, outside the Christian churches (and therefore, of course, often without the perspective that those churches might have offered). This tendency began with the Enlightenment, which can therefore be seen as an inevitable reaction against sixteenth and seventeenth century Augustinianism.

2. MODERN MAN AND CHRISTIAN OBEDIENCE

(a) Modern Man's Criticism of Humility

Humility was criticised in a new way by Descartes, who stressed man's assertion of himself in magnanimity, which Descartes called *générosité*.[33] He was fundamentally concerned with the inalienable ego as the subject of free will. That ego is opposed to any form of servile humility. A new protest based on man's will to power and directed against Christian submissiveness is expressed in Descartes' criticism. Man is seen as in control of himself and the superiority complex of his 'generous' consciousness, inspired by the rediscovery of human grandeur, takes the place of 'Thy will, not mine, be done'.

Spinoza was less inhibited by Christian traditions than Descartes and regarded man's proud assertion of himself as the basis of all virtue. Humility and arrogance he saw as twins; both of them the daughters of an illusory imagination or of dreams.[34] Man, Spinoza taught, had to find his true place and his greatness in the identity of the universe with himself.

Kant was violently opposed to *humilitas spuria* or cringing humility.[35] Although 'phenomenal' man was, for Kant, only an exchangeable value, 'noumenal' man, the person, was an end in itself. Man is rightly conscious of his smallness and real humility when confronted with the law, but he is himself the one who makes and supports that law, with the result that the only proper attitude for him is not one of servile submissiveness, but an assertion of his ethical dignity. He is, after all, autonomous and does not need grace and forgiveness or any form of privilege. He is no one's servant. As the subject of the law he has no need to humiliate himself 'even in the presence of a seraph'. Kant mocked the piety of the psalmist, who declared: 'I am a worm and no man', claiming that 'anyone who makes himself into a worm should not complain if he is trodden on'. Kant was, however, not so naïve as Descartes or Spinoza, neither of whom seemed to be conscious of man's evil intentions. He saw through man's deceitfulness and the injury that it did to man's dignity as an end in itself. He discovered a new form of ethical pride in man's negative experiences of humiliation.

It should not be forgotten in this context that the Enlightenment was preceded by religious wars in Europe. In the light of the deep division in Christianity, both Catholics and Protestants became aware that the political unity of the State could no longer be guaranteed by religion as the basis and expression of social life. If it was to survive as a State, it had to be emancipated from religion, which had acquired a socially disintegrating function. The integrating principle was, from this time onwards, to be enlightened reason, which was in fact a bourgeois or middle-class reason, concerned with what could be calculated and had an exchangeable value in the public sense, with the result that everything else was relegated to the purely private sphere of personal convictions.

According to Kant, the Enlightenment was 'man's exodus from the state in which he has not yet come of age and which is caused by his own guilt', in other words, from his inability to make full use of his own reason without the guidance of others. Authority has to be justified. It has to be capable of being discussed in public. It cannot exist simply on the basis of its 'being there' historically. If it does, it simply produces servants and slaves. If it loses its social plausibility structures, it becomes inhuman coercion. The Enlightenment therefore regarded authority as a relic that had survived from feudalism and the new society as based on a 'contract', which presupposed the equality of all men and their freedom to enter into a contract. The only form of authority that the Enlightenment regarded as valid was the authority of autonomous knowledge or cognitive competence.

Analyses made by B. Groethuysen and others[36] have shown that the history of freedom in the Enlightenment was in fact a very curtailed history of freedom. The specifically class characteristics of the middle-class 'citizen' (that is, not as a *citoyen*, but as a member of a particular economic class) were defined as universally human characteristics (something that had already been done by most of the élitist Greek thinkers in classical antiquity). In other words, specifically middle-class norms were regarded as universally human norms.

This new vision was not so much the result of a new way of looking at life. On the contrary, a new praxis, dominated by the economic principle of exchange, gave rise to the new vision. Life, in other words, took priority over ideas. Even God was made a middle-class citizen in this process, rewarding the good and punishing the bad and thus acting as the guarantor of middle-class society. This also led to a break both with nature and with universal order, which was, of course, not a Stoic action. Nature, the Enlightenment thinkers believed, was dominated by God's natural laws, but man was all-powerful in the human sphere.

God was obliged only to give man his due—in accordance with a kind of contract. Modern man requires guarantees which enable him to know that his efforts do not go unrewarded—the spirit of trade clearly had an effect on religion in the Enlightenment! God's power as it were stopped where human freedom began and God and man were in competition with each other. God became simply the ultimate judge, the 'executive power of middle-class consciousness in the hereafter'.[37] Virtue and ethics were therefore divorced from their relationship with God and truthfulness, honesty and good manners became the foundation of the enlightened way of life. Religion was reduced to ethics and deprived of its mystical and its political potential. The separation of religion from politics, from redemption and liberation, from mysticism and politics is a fundamental characteristic of this individualistic and 'middle-class' religiosity.

Religion also became a separate and private sphere of emotion and sentiment. Man, in his subjectivity, became the measure of all things. This subject, however, was a purely individual self-assertion and not in any way an affirmation of one's fellow-man's freedom in solidarity with him. This middle-class religion therefore eventually became a means by which the people could be made to accept misery in society and injustice caused by other men. The man who was not a middle-class citizen was the victim of this situation and became servile man.

Finally, at a later stage, Nietzsche[38] condemned humility as the product of Judaism and Christianity and a complex of deep resentment. The good news that Jesus proclaimed to slaves became bad news for the powerful. Nietzsche regarded Christian humility as a servile and vindictive distortion of a plebeian consciousness that denies itself in the expectation of eschatological revenge. Magnanimity—in Nietzsche's view, the attitude of the superman—was once again the privilege of a ruling class that created its own values and then made them into universally human norms.

(b) The Christian Criticism of the Privatised Autonomy of Enlightened Reason

Christians are nowadays much more conscious of the fact that God's will can only be known through the mediation of history. They also know that there are dangerous ways of speaking about God's will! If it can only be made known through the medium of man's experiences in the world—a process in which the Christian community and its leaders have to play an interpretative role—then it is true to say that man can never be confronted 'unambiguously' with the will of God.

We may go further and say that ethics are different, as a language game, from religion, which is not simply ethics and cannot be reduced to ethics, despite that fact that there is undeniably an inner connection between religion and the ethical life. An understanding of God and his will must logically be preceded by an understanding of the difference between good and evil. This also means that we should not in the first place define our moral obligations in terms of God's will, but in terms of what is directed towards the dignity of human life. On the other hand, however, the man who believes in God will inevitably and correctly interpret what he regards here and now as worthy of man as an expression of God's will, without sacrificing any of the serious purpose of that will or reducing God himself in a middle-class way to the level of a merely eschatological judge of man's use of his autonomy.

These historical ways of mediating God's will, followed, among others, by those in authority in the Church, add a dialectical dimension to Christian obedience. 'Illegality' can, in certain cases, be interpreted, in a Christian sense, as a higher form of trust in God's Spirit, since there is also a way of trusting God which cannot be traced back to obedience to the authority of the Church. Christians' eyes may have been opened to this by the Enlightenment!

On the other hand, however, the Christian attitude towards authority and obedience may be no more than a protest against the purely cognitive competence of all authority as interpreted by enlightened reason. Authority also has a liberating function with regard to man's true humanity precisely because his critical memory of certain liberating but still unassimilated traditions is an inner, constitutive aspect of his critical reason.[39] Man's state as a subject in solidarity with his fellow-men, which enables him to recognise his fellow-man's freedom and state as a subject, also forms part, in a fully human and theological sense, of the social constitution of the subject.[40] The autonomous middle-class subject is fundamentally criticised from this vantage-point because of his individualistic, utilitarian and non-biblical view of 'autonomous freedom', which acts to others' disadvantage. The principle of exchange, which is reflected in the Enlightenment view of freedom and autonomy, is here revealed, in the light of the Christian tradition, as a diminished form of freedom which in fact makes others (and indeed even the major part of the world's population) victims of a concept of freedom. We are, however, bound to consider, in the difficulties that Christians have with the feudal and patriarchal way of exercising authority (a practice that was justifiably criticised by the Enlightenment), whether the discomfort that some modern Christians experience with regard to religious authority is not connected with a liberal, middle-class view of human freedom and autonomy. All of us who have been brought up in the West are, after all, products of that middle-class culture! In this case, our memory of evangelical freedom has not fully assimilated the latter's criticism of the autarky of the Enlightenment, with the result that we often identify middle-class freedom with evangelical freedom.

Christians should not reject the advances made by the Enlightenment in the process of man's liberation, but they should certainly transcend the diminished freedom of the Enlightenment and, what is more, do this dialectically, by following the direction that J.-B. Metz called that of solidarity of their fellow-man's freedom.[41] It is only if they succeed in doing this that Thomas Aquinas' original view of human grandeur and magnanimity will once again be incorporated into Christian spirituality. If the Enlightenment view of freedom is not dialectically transcended, however, there is a grave danger that a misunderstanding of Thomas's teaching will lead to an increasingly optimistic belief in human progress and a great advance in the ideology of development, thus strengthening and furthering the enslavement of two-thirds of the world's population.

Finally, Christian obedience is above all listening and watching out for the *kairos*, the opportune moment and especially listening obediently to the cry of two-thirds of the world's population for liberation and redemption and then acting in a concrete way in accordance with the voice of God. This is one fundamental form of Christian obedience and one that is derived from the authority of suffering man.

Translated by David Smith

Notes

1. *Nicomachean Ethics* 1124b, 20-1125a.
2. See, for example, A. J. Festugière *La Sainteté* (Paris 1942); ibid. *Contemplation et vie contemplative selon Platon* (Paris 1936); M. Pohlenz *Griechische Freiheit* (Heidelberg 1955).
3. The final version of Aristotle's doctrine on magnanimity is contained in his *Nicomachean Ethics* 1123a, 34-1124b, 6.
4. *op. cit.*, 1099b, 11-14.
5. *op. cit.*, 1167b, 16-1168a, 34; also 1224b, 10-23.
6. *op. cit.*, 1167b, 30-1168a, 34; 1124b, 5-12.
7. *op. cit.*, 1116a, 17-29.
8. *op. cit.*, 1124b, 18-23 and b, 30-31.
9. *op. cit.*, 1169b, 23-28.
10. *op. cit.*, 1169a, 18-20.
11. *Politics* III, 13: 1284a, 3ff.
12. Seneca *De Clementia* 15, 7; see M. Pohlenz *Die Stoa*, 2 vols. (Göttingen 1959).
13. Seneca *Litterae* 4, 1; Epictetus *Dissertationes* II, 16, 11-15.
14. Marcus Aurelius *Meditations (Ta eis heauton)* IX, 40.
15. Epictetus *Dissertationes* IV, 7, 6; Marcus Aurelius *Meditations* XI, 3; Celsus, in Origen *Contra Celsum* VII, 53; VI, 75.
16. P. de Labriolle *La Réaction païenne. Etude sur la polémique anti-chrétienne du premier au sixième siècle* 2nd ed. (Paris 1942), W. Nestle 'Die Haupteinwände des antiken Denkens gegen das Christentum' *Archiv für Religionswissenschaft* 37 (1941) 51-100; E. Dekkers '"Humilitas". Een bijdrage tot de geschiedenis van het begrip "humilitas"' *Horae Monasticae* (Tielt 1947) 67-80; N.-I. Herescu 'Homo-Humus-Humanitas' *Bulletin de l'Association G. Budé* (Paris June 1948) 68ff.

17. Origen *Contra Celsum* VI, 15.
18. *op. cit.,* III, 61.
19. Augustine *Enarr. in Ps.* 31, 18 (*PL* 36, 270); *Tract. in Joh.* 25, c. 16 and 19 (*PL* 35, 1604).
20. Origen *Contra Celsum* VI, 15; III, 62.
21. Augustine *Tract. in Joh.* 25, 16 (*PL* 35, 1604).
22. Bernard *Sermo* V (*PL* 183, 530-532 and 534).
23. *idem. De Consideratione* II, 11 (*PL* 182, 754).
24. *idem. Sermones in Cantica* 34; *Sermones de diversis* 20; *Sermo de conversione ad clericos* 7 (especially *PL* 182, 841).
25. This aspect is neglected in R. Bultot's studies *La Doctrine du mépris du monde* Vols IV-1 and IV-2: *Le XIe siècle* (Louvain and Paris 1963).
26. R. A. Gauthier *Magnanimité. L'idéal de la grandeur dans la philosophie païenne et la théologie chrétienne* (Paris 1951).
27. 'Omnis creatura est tenebra vel falsa vel nihil, *in se* considerata; (hoc dictum) non est intellegendum quod essentia sua sit tenebra vel falsitas, sed quia non habet nec esse nec lucem nec veritatem *nisi ab Alio*', *De Veritate* Q. 8, a. 7 ad 2; 1a-2ae. Q. 109, a. 2 ad 2.
28. According to Augustine, 'ominia sunt bona bonitate divina' (*PL* 40, 30); this was corrected by Thomas as follows: 'Unumquodque dicitur bonum bonitate divina, sicut primo principio exemplari, effectivo et finali totius bonitatis. *Nihilominus* tamen unumquodque dicitur bonum similitudine divinae *sibi inhaerente*, quae est formaliter *sua* bonitas denominans ipsum', 1a, Q. 6, a. 4.
29. See a very acute text in Thomas's commentary on Job, in which man is seen as the ultimate subject. In it, Thomas defends Job's questioning of God: 'It seemed as though a discussion between man and God was improper because God, in his eminence, transcends man. It is important, however, to remember here that truth does not differ according to the person who speaks it; that is why no one speaking the truth can be said to be wrong, whoever his partner in the conversation may be', *Expositio in Job* c. 13, lect. 2.
30. 'Spes, qua quis de Deo confidit, ponitur virtus theologica; . . . sed per fiduciam, quae nunc ponitur pars fortitudinis, homo *habet spem in seipso,* tamen *sub Deo*', 2a-2ae. Q. 128, art. unic., ad 2.
31. See, for example, G. de Lagarde *La Naissance de l'esprit laïque au déclin du moyen âge,* 4 Vols (Paris 1956-1962).
32. *Summa Contra Gentiles* III, 69.
33. Descartes *Traité des passions* III, art. 155-160.
34. Spinoza *Ethica* III, 26, 55; IV, 52, 53, 55, 57.
35. Kant *Der Metaphysik der Sitten. Ethische Elementarlehre* I, Suhrkamp Taschenbuch VIII, ed. W. Weischedel 2nd ed. (Frankfurt 1978) pp. 553-584, especially pp. 568-571.
36. B. Groethuysen *Origines de l'esprit bourgeois en France* (Paris 1927) and, with a more complete critical apparatus, *Die Entstehung der bürgerlichen Welt- and Lebensanschauung in Frankreich,* 2 Vols (Hildesheim and New York 1927 and 1973). Partly dependent on him are, for example, L. Goldmann *Der christliche Bürger und die Aufklärung* (Neuwied 1968) and D. Schellong *Bürgertum und christliche Religion* (Munich 1975). See also *Christianity and the Bourgeoisie, Concilium* 125 (1979) p. 74ff; T. Lemaire *Over de waarde van kulturen* (Baarn 1976).
37. See Groethuysen *Origines* cited in note 36, at p. 123.
38. Nietzsche *Jenseits von Gut und Böse* 260, 261, 267, Kritische Gesamtausgabe, ed. G. Colli and M. Montinari (Berlin 1968) pp. 218-224 and 230-231.
39. J.-B. Metz *Faith in History and Society* (London and New York 1980) *passim.*
40. E. Schillebeeckx *Christ. The Christian Experience in the Modern World* (London and New York 1980) pp. 736-738.
41. J.-B. Metz 'Produktive Ungleichzeitigkeit' *Stichworte zur 'Geistigen Situation der Zeit',* ed. J. Habermas, 2 Vols (Frankfurt 1979) Vol 2 pp. 529-538; see also *ibid.* 'Wenn die Betreuten sich ändern' *Publik-Forum* 13 (27 June 1980) 19-21.

PART II

Theological Foundations

Bas van Iersel

Jesus' Way of Obedience according to Mark's Gospel

INTRODUCTION

IN THE books of the New Testament the words meaning 'obedient' or 'obedience' are used only very occasionally in relation to Jesus of Nazareth. To be precise, they are used not more than three times and then solely in the writings of St Paul or in those influenced by him.

The most important text is, understandably, also the best known. The hymn in Phil. 2:6-11 contains the following verses:

'being born in the likeness of men. And being found in human form he humbled himself and became obedient unto death, even death on a cross' (vv. 7-8).

The last sentence is believed to have been added to the existing hymn by Paul himself.

The second text appears in the letter to the Romans and reads: 'For as by one man's disobedience many were made sinners, so by one man's obedience many will be made righteous' (Rom. 5:19). And finally, there is a passage in the letter to the Hebrews: 'Although he was a Son, he learned obedience through what he suffered' (Hebr. 5:8).

It is noticeable that all three texts refer, either directly or indirectly, to the suffering and death of Jesus and to what these mean for mankind. But these are the only direct references. The noun ὑπακοή (hupakoê) appears twice, the adjective ὑπήκοος (hupêkoos) once and the verb not at all. There are, however, other sayings which also have some connection with the concept of obedience, such as Jesus' words in Gethsemane: 'Yet not what I will, but what thou wilt'. We are, therefore, clearly making a mistake if we think we can restrict ourselves to passages which contain words formed from a single basic stem. We must look further.

Dismissing one restriction we are soon faced with another. Jesus' obedience is referred to in so many diverse ways in the various books of the New Testament, that it is not possible to deal with all those texts without losing oneself in trivialities which would be better left unread and, therefore, unwritten. That is the reason why this article will deal with only one gospel text. The advantage of this is that we have before us one consistent image of Jesus, the disadvantage is that this represents only one of the many images. However, this creates no serious problem, because even the complete New Testament does not present us with a complete and perfect image of Jesus as an obedient person, and of what this means for us. Of the four gospels that of Mark has been chosen for two reasons both of which are somewhat trivial. First, it would be very difficult to do full justice to a long gospel text in a short article such as this. Second, it fits better into my present teaching and research commitments.

Jesus' words in Gethsemane will serve as a starting point. The version which first comes to mind is that of Luke, whereas Mark writes in 14:36: 'Abba, Father, all things are possible to thee; remove this cup from me; yet not what I will, but what thou wilt'. Is this a statement of servility, or setting aside his own initiative, creative plans and ideas? Does it appear to be blind obedience which, according to present western belief, is contrary to the dignity of man? We shall see. In order to do so, it is necessary to consider how in Mark's gospel the business of God is diametrically opposed to that of man.

1. GOD'S WILL AND MAN'S WILL

The statement that God's will is different from that of man, and that it would be better if man adjusted his will to that of God is sometimes made with polemical overtones, and sometimes without. It is definitely polemical, when Mark relates how Jesus, who has finally left his native Nazareth and his relations, reacts on being told that his mother and brothers are trying to contact him. He replies: 'Who are my mother and my brethren?' And looking at those who are seated around him, he says: 'Here are my mother and my brethren. Whoever does the will of God is my brother, and sister, and mother' (3:33-35). It remains unclear, however, what exactly the alternative to doing the will of God is. Is it following one's own will or that of others, is it not doing the will of God or perhaps not doing anything at all? What is plain is that carrying out the will of God is a characteristic of Jesus himself as well as of all those whom he acknowledges to be related to him as members of a new family.

Opposing those who relate themselves in this way to Jesus is a group of people who appear to be adversaries: scribes and Pharisees, Herodians, chief priests and elders of the people. Of the opposition Jesus repeats what is written in Isaiah: 'teaching as doctrines the precepts of men' (7:7), and he accuses them: 'You leave the commandment of God, and hold fast the tradition of men' (7:8); 'You have a fine way of rejecting the commandment of God, in order to keep your tradition' (7:9); and 'thus making void the word of God through your tradition which you hand on' (7:13). I have quoted these three passages in full for more than one reason. First, to point out how often within a few lines of text the same theme is repeated. Second, to show the climax in the text. What in the beginning is called 'the tradition of men' changes into 'your tradition' and finally into 'your tradition which you hand on'. It is, therefore, clear that God's will is opposed by one's own will as well as that of man. Just as the followers of Jesus are characterised by the fact that they are carrying out God's will, so it is typical of his opponents to renounce God's will in favour of precepts of their own making, disguised as rules which derive their authority from ancient tradition. Jesus, therefore, calls them 'hypocrites' (7:6) when they accuse his disciples of not observing the traditional customs which have been in force as of old (7:5).

There is another passage in Mark where they are called hypocrites, i.e., when followers of Herod and Pharisees ask Jesus: 'Teacher, we know that you are true, and care for no man; for you do not regard the position of men, but truly teach the way of God. Is it lawful to pay taxes to Caesar, or not? Should we pay them, or should we not?' (12:14). The use of the word 'true' only reinforces their hypocrisy and, as is usual with hypocrites, their words are partly true, partly untrue. That Jesus defers to no one is only true in as far as he is unaffected by what others think and say of him. He does not behave in accordance with their will. But it is untrue if they mean to say that Jesus has no concern for his fellow-men. The opposite rather is the case. When these opponents say that Jesus teaches the way of God in all honesty without taking man's position into account, it is completely in keeping with what we have read in chapter 7. Mark allows those who prefer man's law to God's will to give a spiritual description of Jesus, their opponent.

What is related about Jesus and Peter in the middle of the gospel is, in this connection, of particular importance, although the word 'obedience' is not used and no explicit mention of God's will is made. It starts with Jesus questioning his disciples: 'Who do men say that I am?' (8:27). The reply naturally does not go beyond the prevailing rumours: 'John the Baptist . . . Elijah . . . one of the prophets' (8:28). What the disciples themselves believe goes, in principle, no further either, as is shown when Peter answers 'the Christ' (8:29). As yet man does not have the appropriate answer. The exact answer as to who Jesus is comes to his disciples from heaven: 'This is my beloved Son; listen to him' (9:7). But that answer will become known only after the reader has been told about an unusually fierce discussion between Peter and Jesus regarding the latter's death. Jesus accuses Peter of choosing not the side of God but that of man. Peter seems to have turned from being a disciple into becoming an opponent. He is a turncoat because he takes the side of man against God. It also becomes plain for the first time that whoever is not servile to man is bound to be delivered into the hands of men, as it says in 9:31. And whoever is delivered into their hands knows that he can expect no mercy. He who, like Peter, finds this a reason for changing course makes a wrong choice. He chooses the side of man and is against God.

If Jesus is *destined* to suffer (8:31), it does not necessarily mean that he submits himself to his destiny without regard to his own will, or that he subjects himself, without making a deliberate choice, to what has been intended for him by the one he calls 'Abba'. His obedience is no servility. This is made abundantly clear in a passage of Mark's gospel preceding the story of Jesus' death. Passers-by and opponents are in unison. The first shout: 'Aha! You who would destroy the temple and build it in three days, save yourself, and come down from the cross' (15:29-30). And the opponents jeer mockingly: 'He saved others; he cannot save himself. Let the Christ, the king of Israel, come down now from the cross, that we may see and believe' (15:31-32). It seems plausible to assume that the reader, however, knows that Jesus is quite capable of coming down from that cross. He has read about many more astonishing events. For instance, that Jesus overpowered a whole legion of demons, saved a man possessed from their clutches and sent the demons into a herd of pigs and drowned them (5:1-20). Would he not be able then to remove himself from the cross and to overcome a handful of soldiers? If it does not happen, the reason is not that he would be unable to do so but that he has no wish to do so. It is a confirmation of his choice: 'Yet not what I will, but what thou wilt'.

However, there remains one question. If there is such a fundamental difference between what Jesus might wish and God's will, and if that difference also exists between God's command and man's will, how is it that Jesus knows God's will?

2. A COMMAND FROM HEAVEN?

The question of how Jesus knows God's will is not answered in Mark in the way that might be expected and corresponds to conventional ideas. Jesus is deemed to have had contact with God in such a manner as has never been granted to any man, namely through a process of inward seeing and hearing that lasted continuously and left him in no doubt as to what he had to do. However, there is no indication whatsoever of this in the image of Jesus that Mark depicts. That this contact would be continuous and all-embracing is even contradicted in 13:32, where Jesus says that not even the Son knows the day or the hour of the end. How then has Jesus, according to Mark, learned of God's will?

It appears to me that a definite answer can be found on the first page of Mark's gospel. This contains the story of how it all began, of what preceded Jesus' preaching in Galilee (1:14-15), of recruiting supporters and disciples (1:16-20) and of helping people in distress (1:21-34). It is true that in the very beginning a voice sounds from heaven, but this does not reveal to Jesus what he is to do. The words 'Thou art my beloved Son; with thee I am well pleased' (1:11), rather create the impression that they are a confirmation of what has happened before. What then has Jesus been doing previously? Exactly what people from Judea and Jerusalem had been doing before him, namely listening to the voice of John the Baptist and queueing up to confess their sins and to be baptised. When his time came Jesus was also baptised by John the Baptist in the river Jordan.

One can, therefore, conclude that Jesus listened to the voice of one crying in the wilderness and, in reply to his appeal, changed his course of life. He has left his native Nazareth and his brothers and sisters in order to devote himself to his life's work. Whether this is described as a calling or as a conversion makes little difference. What matters is that he has recognised God's voice in the message of John the Baptist. It would mean that, according to Mark, Jesus has no other or more privileged way of knowing God's will than have others, i.e., through a human voice.

That this is not a whimsical idea is surprisingly shown in another passage of Mark's gospel. In 11:27-28 the chief priests, scribes and elders ask Jesus by what authority he carries out his activities, particularly in the Temple. Jesus replies with a question of his own: 'I will ask you a question; answer me, and I will tell you by what authority I do these things. Was the baptism of John from heaven or from men? Answer me.' (11:29-30). Jesus receives no reply and so says no more. However, the answer to his opponents is clearly implied. John has been sent by God. His baptism as well as his message come from God. Jesus has heard God's voice in that of John; God's will has been revealed to Jesus through a human voice. The change, rejected by his opponents (11:31), but accepted by Jesus, has created such an evident and irreversible conflict between them that Jesus feels justified in acting against them like that. Yet, when a voice from heaven confirms that Jesus has understood the message of John the Baptist and has done what it requested of him, this voice is apparently not considered an authentication in the eyes of his opponents, even though Jesus points out to them indirectly through a parable that the one whose death they are plotting (11:18) is considered by God to be his Son (12:1-12).

According to Mark, listening to the voice of God is for Jesus the same as accepting the Baptist's message. It is no surprise, therefore, that the preaching of Jesus is, to a certain extent, a continuation of what John the Baptist has been saying. Both are concerned with repentance (1:4, 15). It is hardly more surprising that Mark draws a parallel between Jesus and John which is apparent when the author describes the arrest of John the Baptist in 1:14 (the word 'tradere'—παραδίδωμι (paradidomi) in regard to people is reserved in future only for Jesus 3:19; 9:31; 10:33; 14:10, 11, 18, 21, 41, 42, 44; 15:1, 10, 15, and for Jesus' disciples 13:9, 10, 12). It is also worth noting that Mark's gospel contains a kind of passion story about John, similar to that of Jesus (6:17-29) and that the resurrection of the Baptist is mentioned (6:14-16) albeit only through the mouth of Herod.

This parallel with John the Baptist, however, is not followed through when Mark writes about the activities of Jesus. John's activities are restricted to preaching (1:2-8), denouncing (6:18) and baptising (1:4, 5, 9). Nowhere does Mark mention that Jesus is baptising. On the other hand a great deal more detail is related about Jesus than about John. Jesus performs great and remarkable deeds. The striking thing is that he carries them out not only without any demonstrative purpose, in fact to the contrary, but not even on his own initiative. The stereotyped image of a Jesus who sets out doing good to demonstrate who he is and what God wants to reveal to mankind is not to be found in Mark. This is also true with regard to the image of a Jesus who performs miracles to prove his point and his identity. Whenever Jesus takes the initiative it is in connection with preaching the Good News (1:14-15; 1:38), with persuading people to become his followers (1:16-20; 2:14, 17—when the initiative is taken by someone else, the result is quite different 5:18-19; 10:17-22), and with attacking abuses and opponents (3:1-15; 11:15-17; 12:35-40).

Nowhere is Jesus seen to be seeking out the sick, the poor or the possessed, as though he were driven on by an inward voice or a heavenly mission. He just meets them on his way (1:23; 3:1), they come to him (1:40; 3:10; 5:2, 27-28; 10:47) or, in the case of children, their parents come to Jesus (5:22; 7:25-26), he is taken to them (1:30; 5:22-23) or they are brought to him (1:32; 2:3; 6:55-56; 7:32; 8:22; 9:17).

The same pattern can also be discovered in the two stories concerning the feeding of the multitude, in as far as they start with people being hungry (6:35; 8:2) which moves Jesus to do something for them. These kind of stories usually start with a request made to Jesus (1:30-40; 2:3-4; 4:38; 5:23, 27; 7:26, 32; 8:22; 9:18; 10:47-48). It can be stated without exaggeration that Jesus comes to the aid of people almost only when an appeal is made to him or when a situation requires it. If in these circumstances he is responding to a voice, then this voice is the voice of *people* pleading with him. If it is true that Jesus receives a command from heaven, it is transmitted to him through human voices which can be heard also by others, and not through a special and privileged enlightening message.

3. PEOPLE AND 'MAN'

The conclusion of the preceding paragraph is, in the first instance, difficult to square with what has been said before, i.e., that in Mark's gospel there is a clear contrast between God's command and the will of man. However, if we read the text properly and consider the terminology used, the two statements appear to be in no way contradictory. The contradiction stems from the fact that *we* summarise a number of stories in a general conclusion saying that Jesus hears God's will in what people tell and ask him. When we talk about 'people' we ought to realise that the actual story is always about one or more concrete persons, individual characters. Sometimes these persons are described very fully, on other occasions the information given about them is scant. Sometimes it only says 'a man with an unclean spirit' (1:23; 5:2), or 'a man who had a withered hand' (3:1), 'demoniac' (3:15), 'paralytic' (2:3), 'a man who was deaf' (7:32), 'a blind man' (8:22). Elsewhere more details are given about such a person, e.g., that it is Simon's mother-in-law who has gone to bed with fever (1:30), that it is the little daughter of a pagan woman from Syrophoenicia who is ill (7:25-26), or the 12-year-old daughter of Jairus, one of the synagogue officials (5:22, 42), or Bartimaeus, a blind beggar, sitting at the side of the road (10:47). In the case of a woman who has suffered from a haemorrhage a great deal of the history of her illness is told (5:27-28). Of John the Baptist, whose message is really at the origin of all that Jesus does, more information is given than can be summarised in a few lines. In other words, these are all people but never 'man' through whom Jesus learns God's will.

That Mark makes this distinction consciously is clear from the fact that, with one exception (8:24), he uses the expression 'homines'—'ἀνθρώποι' always in a derogatory sense (7:7, 8, 21; 8:27, 33; 9:31; 11:30, 32). This is very obvious, not only from the three passages 7:1-23; 8:27-33 and 11:27-33 which have been briefly discussed before, but also from the announcement of the suffering of Jesus in 9:31, when we compare this text with other passages announcing the suffering and death of the Son of man. In 9:31 we read: 'The Son of man will be delivered into the hands of men, and they will kill him.' If it is not immediately clear who 'men' are, other texts such as 8:31 ('be rejected by the elders and the chief priests and the scribes'), 10:33 ('the Son of man will be delivered to the chief priests and the scribes') and 14:41 ('the Son of man is betrayed into the hands of sinners') give a definitive explanation. It follows that 'men' are the opponents of Jesus who seek his death. When Mark uses the word 'men' it does not have a neutral, let alone favourable, meaning, but clearly has a derogatory connotation.

More important, however, is that in revealing Jesus' opponents and identifying them with 'men' Mark gives us an insight into two types of obedience. To understand this it is necessary to examine more closely a number of contrasts between Jesus and his opponents, as they occur before the story of the passion. Already in 1:22 the first contrast is evident. Jesus teaches with authority, unlike the scribes. This means that the scribes derive their authority from the link they have with ancient traditions. Jesus, however, exercises direct and personal authority. He has no need to rely on predecessors. This authority manifests itself in the apparent control he exercises over the unclean spirits (1:27). The scribes, who have come down from the city where Jesus' death is being plotted and where it will take place (3:22), explain this by saying that Jesus has entered into an alliance with a more powerful spirit, the prince of devils (3:22). Jesus makes it quite clear that they refuse to acknowledge that it is the *Holy Spirit* who has been present and working in him since his baptism in the River Jordan, not, as they claim, an *unclean spirit* (1:10; 3:29). They falsify reality and blaspheme against the Holy Spirit (3:29-30). And as Mark's story develops, the reader gradually begins to realise that these scribes and other authorities from Jerusalem are the very ones who themselves work hand in glove with the prince of devils. It goes without saying that the opponents of Jesus also deny him the authority to forgive sins (2:1-12) and strongly object to his associating with sinners and tax collectors (2:16). The observance of the sabbath is an issue that particularly highlights the existing conflict (2:18-3:6). The opponents are depicted as people who consider it more important to observe the sabbath regulations than to help their fellow-men in distress. Jesus reverses this attitude (2:27) and challenges them. He makes a point of restoring, on a sabbath, the use of his hand to a handicapped man whilst they are in the synagogue (3:2-5). He motivates his actions by asking his opponents: 'Is it lawful on the sabbath to do good or to do harm, to save life or to kill?' (3:4). The story itself makes it impossible to see this solely or mainly as an abstract principle. By his words Jesus also reveals the character of his opponents. Subsequently, they leave the synagogue and hatch a plot with the Herodians to do away with Jesus (3:6). The sabbath, which Jesus uses to do good, they abuse by planning Jesus' death.

This brings to light how completely different the obedience of Jesus is from that of his opponents. Jesus' opponents are obedient to tradition, to what has been laid down, which leads to rigid repetition, routine, constraint and lack of freedom. Jesus' obedience is much more related to the challenge of the moment. It is not reproductive but creative, it embodies human liberty and it contributes to freedom, health and happiness. It is definitely not submissiveness and blind servility to a way of life programmed in advance, as many believe. On the contrary, on every occasion he has to make a new decision, a new choice, because his way of life is not governed by unalterable rules laid down by tradition but by the needs of actual people which continually face him with different challenges. Jesus is not dominated by 'man', i.e., by the conventions of society, but by God's will. This reveals an even deeper contrast, because Jesus' God is not a God of the dead, but of the living (12:27). Particularly in the story of the healing of the man with the withered hand (3:1-6) and in the reference to Jesus' death (3:6), it is clearly shown in which sense Jesus is obedient to the God of the living. His obedience is concerned with life, with well-being and salvation. The obedience of his opponents, however, is related to death and destruction, as is apparent from the manner in which they behave towards Jesus.

For Jesus it means that, although his life is not directed by an all-dominating will of God, he cannot follow any arbitrary course of action either. Obedience to God means for Jesus that he is governed by a fundamental attitude inclined towards salvation and healing, and expressing his belief that fulfilling the first commandment on its own is insufficient and should be accompanied by the second: 'You shall love your neighbour as yourself' (12:31).

4. OBEDIENT UNTO DEATH

Jesus' obedience is not passive, it is not submissive servility, but it expresses itself in activity and creativity. It may not appear to be that way in the part of Mark's gospel that we rightly call the passion. From the moment he is arrested in the garden, where he literally is delivered into the hands of men, he is pushed around. The course of events during Jesus' last days seems to be described perfectly by the text Philip uses in Acts 8:32-35:

'As a sheep led to the slaughter
or a lamb before its shearer is dumb,
So he opens not his mouth'   (Isa. 53:7).

There are some who refer, in my opinion wrongly, to these words in Isaiah when mentioning Jesus' silence in front of the high priest and Pilate (14:61; 15:5).

The impression of passivity we may be given proves to be quite wrong, if we read the text properly and if we start with the story of the passion in the correct place, namely in 8:27, when Jesus sets out with the twelve and makes it clear to them that the journey will end in suffering, rejection, death and resurrection (8:31). For the first time in Mark we come across the word 'must' ('oportet'—'δεῖ'). What is to happen to the Son of man is inevitable. But what kind of inevitability is this? Is it the will of a repressive God, that of an inescapable destiny? We shall return to this issue later. From the text in 8:31, where the chief priests and scribes are mentioned, it is evident to the attentive reader that the journey leads to Jerusalem (10:32-33). Jesus is going because there he is to be delivered into the hands of men (9:31). However, it is not happening in conflict with his own will. To a certain extent, he even seems to co-operate. Not only does he go to Jerusalem of his own free will, but he also challenges and provokes his opponents by entering the city and the Temple triumphantly (11:1-11) and by chasing the vendors out of the holy place (11:15-19). He tries to make it clear to them in a parable what they are actually doing (12:1-12), he vaguely indicates that he knows the one who is to betray him (14:12-21), and then he meets him courageously (14:42) after fighting an inward struggle in the solitude of Gethsemane (14:32-41). From the moment he is delivered into the hands of 'men' he loses the initiative. All that he has left are his voice and his word. He chooses to be silent in front of the high priest until he is asked whether he is the Christ, the Son of the Blessed One (14:61). The answer is unambiguous, straightforward and affirmative. But he adds that he, the Son of man, will pronounce judgment over his opponents when he comes again (14:62).

The fact that Jesus is co-operative in the face of death should not be interpreted as an aspiration to a mystical experience of suffering or of death, or as a sign of his being tired of life. This is quite clear from what happens in the garden of Gethsemane (14:32-42). It should be associated with what we read in 10:45: 'For the Son of man also came not to be served but to serve, and to give his life as a ransom for many'. This should not make us immediately think of a theology of redemption in which debt to God can only be expiated by blood. The word 'ransom' rather refers to an enemy wanting to be paid. In the olden days one might think of the master of a slave or a general holding prisoners of war; nowadays we are more inclined to think of terrorists demanding money in exchange for the lives of hostages. I am of the opinion that in 10:45 we ought not to think of God as the one who has determined the ransom and is waiting to be paid. It is rather Jesus' opponents who demand his life (Mark 3:6 onward), and it is not accidental that he dies a violent death. He is murdered by his enemies. When by going to Jerusalem Jesus seeks them out and challenges them, he does it because he cannot but oppose and obstruct his opponents. If he were to cease fighting them, he would renege on the essence of his message (i.e., that the moment of salvation has arrived and henceforth people should change their way of life) and the fundamental motive of all his actions. This also explains why the word 'must' is used in 8:31, when Jesus and his disciples set out for Jerusalem. This 'must' refers to God's will which directs Jesus' way of life and to which he wants to be obedient. If that 'must' also refers to Jesus' death on the cross, it is not because the God of the living makes an exception for his Son Jesus, but because there are men who resist him to the end and do not flinch from murdering him.

Of particular importance for the reader is that Jesus does not set out for Jerusalem on his own. He is accompanied by his disciples. The story of the journey, therefore, also acts as a lesson for the reader who considers himself a disciple of Jesus. This lesson tends to change him from being a blind man (8:22) into someone who sees and follows Jesus on his way (10:52). The meaning of being a real follower of Jesus is explained in the conversation between Jesus and Peter after the first announcement of Jesus' passion and in the subsequent sayings (8:31-9:1). The words quoted earlier are important in this respect: 'Get behind me, Satan! For you are not on the side of God, but of men' (8:33). He who really wants to be a follower of Jesus—whether or not he is called Peter—is told to renounce himself and to take up his cross, i.e., like Jesus he must give up his life (8:34-35). We are inclined, together with Luke (9:23), to explain these words in a figurative sense. I am of the opinion that they must be understood literally. They refer to Christians who, just like Jesus, have been brought before the court and are coerced into denying their faith, renouncing Jesus and thus saving their lives (cf. Mark 13:9-13; 4:17; 10:30).[1] He who yields will save his mortal life but lose his real life. He who defies death, as Jesus does, will truly live. It does not follow that development of oneself is being rejected and the expression of one's personality is being replaced by the denial of it. If one understands these words in that way, one forgets that they are said on the way to Jerusalem, the place where Jesus is to be tried. This Jerusalem is not the heavenly Jerusalem of which the Apocalypse speaks. For those who follow Jesus it is the place where they are to be persecuted. If one is tried and faced with the choice, one must be prepared to suffer torture and execution for one's belief in Jesus. In other words, obedience unto death for Jesus' followers does not represent an attitude of contempt for life or oneself. Death in this case occurs through execution on the cross or through other means. A Christian need not necessarily seek it. He knows, however, that his acting and speaking as a Christian may put him in such a position that one day the established powers and interested parties will come into action against him. This is not always and everywhere relevant. In the country in which I am writing this article it is not a reality. In other countries, however, where this article may be read it could well be a real possibility. It is true that nowadays Christians are very seldom dragged before the courts to renounce Jesus, but if they draw consequences from their belief in Jesus which those in power do not like, they are abducted, tortured, deported, stripped of their rights, assassinated in secret as enemies of the governing régime or as elements dangerous to the State.

To remain obedient to the way of Jesus is the opposite of passivity or servility. Even though the gospel of Mark says that anyone who wants to be first must be slave to all (10:44), this does not mean a servility of the boot-licker, or the subjugated, of the one who lives by commands.

It is rather an expression of the utmost freedom which transforms people into such principled creatures that they do not call a halt even when their actions may lead to loss of freedom, to torture and even to execution.

Translated by W. M. P. Kruyssen

Notes

1. Further details can be found in B. van Iersel 'The Gospel according to St Mark—Written for a Persecuted Community?' *Nederlands Theologisch Tijdschrift* 34 (1980) 15-36.

Pierre de Locht

Freedom of Obedience to the Spirit in the Church

WHEN THEY were accused by the High Priest and the Council of disobeying the formal injunction against teaching in the name of Jesus, Peter and the apostles said: 'We must obey God rather than men' (Acts 5:29).

This appeal to an authority higher than any human court of judgment ('the Holy Spirit whom God has given to those who obey him', Acts 5:32) has recurred throughout all the stages of Christianity in its twenty centuries of development. The Spirit empowered the martyrs, and all those men and women who ardently defended their commitment to the gospel wherever the faith was threatened. But it is usually in regard to temporal powers that deny or persecute Christians and the Church that this relationship with the Spirit is invoked ('And we are witnesses to these things and so is the Holy Spirit . . .', Acts 5:32) which allows one to prefer God's to men's authority. But does a choice of this kind have any meaning within the Church itself? Does Christian obedience itself acknowledge and experience this problematical and painful tension between established norms and the promptings of the Spirit?

'True freedom is a privileged sign of the divine image in man' says *Gaudium et Spes* (§17). Nevertheless the declaration of Vatican II on religious freedom confined itself almost exclusively to those aspects of that freedom which have to do with the secular powers: '. . . more and more people are demanding that men should exercise fully their own judgment and a responsible freedom in their actions and should not be subject to the pressure of coercion but be inspired by a sense of duty. At the same time they are demanding constitutional limitation of the powers of government to prevent excessive restriction of the rightful freedom of individuals and associations' (*Dignitatis humanae*, §1).

1. ORIGINS OF DISOBEDIENCE

'Contestation' or civil disobedience has hardly received a good press in our various communities and societies. It is perceived as negative, even as destructive, by the powers that be, as well as by all those who tend to support a stabilised society that has often been achieved with difficulty. The Catholic Church is far from rejecting this view of such disobedience; indeed, in the words of Paul VI, it has said that 'there is no room for "conscientious objection" which destroys obedience in the Church' (Speech to the Tribunal of the Sacred Rota, 4 February 1977. Cf. *Doc. cath.*, 6 March 1977, col. 207).

Surely this is a somewhat one-sided understanding of conscientious objection and disobedience, one which refuses to acknowledge the conditions which give rise to them even within Christian obedience? It is appropriate to describe one of the forms of this disobedience which is most often met with.

It is wrong to suppose that contestation necessarily arises within a psychologically disturbed mind, on a basis of maladjustment and rebellion. On the contrary, it may be found within a sincere and wholehearted commitment to the Church's teaching and discipline.

In contact with actual experience, or problems posed by cultural change, or as a result of more detailed research—often as a result of all these different factors—one begins to discern to some extent new aspects of the reality one encounters or the message that one is living or teaching. It might be some aspect which until then one has not taken sufficiently into consideration, or some dimension of existence whose importance one had all but ignored, or some value that one had allowed to become obscured; this aspect, value and dimension begin gradually to appear in a new light. This new awareness is seen as postive and enriching; it is not destructive but offers new values or shows old ones as they really are. If one shares one's new vision with others whom one finds sympathetic, its meaning for one becomes more precise and profound, and its productivity is confirmed.

Nevertheless, experience shows that when one shares with others on a somewhat larger scale some approach that one found constructive and fulfilling, surprisingly enough it provokes opposition. It soon becomes clear that for those who have not experienced such a new awareness from within, what gets attention and consideration is mainly what the particular viewpoint has called in question, rather than the to some extent new enlightenment and values that it brings with it. However positive the new awareness may have been for those who experienced the awakening, it becomes destructive in the eyes of those for whom the *status quo* is the main norm of reference.

This kind of rejection is wholly understandable. Those who have not as yet been able to appreciate the meaning and possible richness of the new awareness, see first of all what it is going to destroy. The cold shoulder some people and often authority give the new concept, however off-putting and painful it may be, can prove valuable. It makes one go into greater detail, and exhaustively probe an insight which needs the searchlight of criticism. Every discovery is multivalent; opposition to it can prove beneficial, on condition that it is advanced in an atmosphere of respect and openness. The main acceptation of the verb 'contest' in pre-1968 French usage is to argue or plead on the basis of evidence (see the *Petit Robert Dictionary*). In many cases, however, this possibility is hardly available; contestation is not accepted in its real meaning and those who undertake it are rejected or disqualified.

2. TWO DIMENSIONS OF LOYALTY

In such a case one is faced with the dilemma of divided loyalties: loyalty to the community to which one belongs and of which one remains an accountable part, and to that hierarchical authority whose due respect one never neglects; but loyalty as well to that new awareness and to the existential reality and the reality of individual liberation which it brings with it. In this movement to and fro between two indispensable dimensions of loyalty, which should one obey? Should one surrender personal judgment in the name of some specific form of 'Christian' submission? There are probably many people who have never been faced with such a dilemma of conscience regarding not relatively secondary aspects but questions which they see as crucial for human life and for the gospel message. But the trial is excruciating only for those who have a deep and vital attachment to the Church.

Some people resolve this dilemma by surrendering themselves unconditionally to the decisions of authority. That seems to them to be the only loyal and faithful course possible. The spirituality of the individual Christian and much more of the priest and of the religious has often centred upon this ascetic self-surrender in the name of the evangelical counsels.

Others, in good conscience too, think that they should accept a form of loyalty that is probably somewhat more complex. After inquiring into personal values of self-denial, humble submission, and renunciation of one's own right of judgment, they come to ask whether the demands of the search for truth, the situation of the individuals in question, and the good of the institution do not require that they should continue to say what they think is true. Is it possible for those who do not or do not any longer agree with the official teaching on this or that particular point to remain silent, when real human situations are in question, and when people are not acknowledged to be truly and honourably engaged with what they are doing with their lives? Is this silence favourable to the Church which, under the pressure of tradition and of fear of the unknown, like any institution runs the danger of not admitting the exigencies of life? Contestation and even disobedience can surely be, in the Church too, a means of criticism and of self-development for the established order, a stirring of truth and a thrust into the future?

Such people think that it is not enough to consider only the ascetic aspect of obedience but that they should look at its repercussions on the operation of the institution. It is the good of all which is really in question. If the entire community must be able to count on the loyalty of its members in order to achieve its goals, it is just as necessary for it to experience differences and the surprise of new demands and healthy tensions to be expected in a living process. Moreover, if the structures of the Church no longer possess means of true universal and responsible participation, we must ask if silence and submission are really the only attitudes proper to loyalty and obedience. For instance, in the case of re-married divorced persons or homosexuals or others whose experiences often affect them urgently, should we be satisfied with very unsatisfactory individual solutions which can even prove debilitating, touched as they are with condescension and secretiveness? The serious dichotomy between accepted and recommended practice and 'principles' which are still presented as the ideal, even when they no longer possess any inspiring value, is scandalous for many and disruptive of moral order. Only institutional questioning can help to redress this moral disarray.

3. SERVICE OF THE CHURCH

When we remember that many major questions are not subject to open discussion in the Church, that arguments drawn from the 'unanimous teaching of the pope and the bishops' and appeal to submission constitute the only answers to major demands of human existence; and that many people are neither heard nor acknowledged in terms of their lived reality; we have to ask if silence and solidarity are the only means of sharing the common good?

Some people think that their very commitment to the Church and to its magisterium demands that they should continue relentlessly, whatever the circumstances, as prudently but as forcefully as the situation requires, to state questions which echo those problems experienced by a great number of Catholic Christians. To stop self-expression means reinforcing a form of behaviour which is seriously injurious both to the teaching of the Church and to the ecclesial conscience of Christians, and consists in closing oneself up in proofs which are never open to new analysis, and to rejecting without any contradictory study any especially thorny problems. But authority is not necessarily the best-equipped means of perceiving the urgency of contemporary problems. *Inter alia* that is the case with marital sex which has necessarily remained outside the direct experiential understanding of a hierarchy and clergy recruited solely from among male celibates.

The common good and the healthy exercise of authority require that realities which are partly new or understood in hitherto uncomprehended respects should not be brushed aside, even if they happen to disturb established modes of thought, standard evidence and authorised teaching. Surely all Christians should contribute to the present-day understanding of the gospel message and share in the continuing growth to maturity of the Church's teaching?

Rather than hide in a silence which refutes a many-sided life of faith, and rather than give into the temptation of leaving the Church out of tedium or annoyance, surely one recommendable form of loyalty and obedience would be to testify to one's worries and discoveries in a firm call to confrontation and dialogue? Some people do that, often after a somewhat difficult and painful journey. They experience this tension calmly, without strain, as a normal and healthy demand from a Church which is constantly searching for a better understanding of the Good News of Jesus Christ.

In their eyes, loyal contestation, far from being a lack of commitment or an indication of disloyalty, becomes a constitutive element of obedience. Are they wrong, and if so in what way?

4. WHOM DOES THE CHRISTIAN OBEY IN THE CHURCH?

This experience of transgression which is lived as a demand of loyalty and obedience, evokes various questions which are essential for the Christian and for the community. Let me try (not, of course, to resolve them but) to attempt a first approach to a solution.

(a) Each is disposed to the common good

The goal of obedience is not individual sanctification but the viability and fruitfulness of social life. Renunciation and asceticism, which the practice of obedience can involve, does not constitute the proper goal of obedience; it is only a consequence which may indeed be partially unfortunate.

Obedience is not only the virtue of the 'subordinate'. More precisely, everyone, whatever the position he or she occupies in the community, should be actively concerned for the whole. Everyone is in some way 'subordinated' to the common good. And even though the positions and decisions of authority normally constitute an especially qualified expression of social goals and of the common good, that does not mean that they are the only expression of those goals and of that good. The position occupied by the authorities with its incontestable possibilities of insight constitutes its limits and dead-ends. There is an essential complementarity of different judgments which must take effect in a society if the good of each and the health of the whole are to thrive.

(b) A Church in the world

Because of its nature and its specific goals, the Church does not escape the usual exigencies of social life and the exercise of authority.

It is often said, in order to dismiss the analysis of inadequacies of ecclesial functioning and especially the demands of the ordinary Church—the grass-roots—for a share in the common responsibility, that the Church is not a democracy. Do those who say so mean that the true reality and goal of the Church impose on it a mode of operation which is removed from the common conditions of human life? But in the course of its history the ecclesial institution has been very closely inspired by existing régimes such as the Roman Empire and later western-type monarchies. It is right and proper to stay like that in a world where attempts are being made, though not without difficulty, to awaken universal participation in communual responsibilities? Do the extreme slowness of the securing of structures of true participation in the Church, the refusal to allow anything other than consultative status to the various advisory bodies assembled since the Council, and the increasing centralisation in so many areas (made much more effective by modern means of communication), lead us to suppose that the specific nature of the Church forces it to adopt a mode of operation closer to that proper to totalitarian régimes than to approaches to real democracy? Is that what is demanded by loyalty to life and to the message of Jesus Christ?

Instead of stating that the institutional Church cannot, under threat of losing its identity, model its organisation on other human societies, we have to ask why it has committed itself to one particular type of operation and does all it can to stay like that. A fundamental institutional analysis and precise theological reflection are necessary to reveal what is the result of mere contingencies of the Church's history as opposed to the very essence of its specific mission. This kind of discernment, dependent of course on specialist research work, is proper to the whole church community, both the magisterium and grass-roots Christians. 'The whole body of the faithful who have an anointing that comes from the holy one (see 1 John 2:20, 27) cannot err in matters of belief. This characteristic is shown in the supernatural appreciation of the faith of the whole people, when, "from the bishops to the last of the faithful", they manifest a universal consent in matters of faith and morals' (*Lumen gentium*, § 12). Why should the disposition of ecclesial tasks be outside this universal manifestation of consent?

(c) Loyalty to the Spirit 'who bloweth where he listeth'

Under its usual conditions, loyalty arises from a constructive tension between two poles: individual responsibility (the will, understanding of the common good, commitment . . .) and the law, of which legitimate authority is the normal expression and guarantor. In any case of uncertainty or conflict between the responsible freedom of individuals and the directives of authority, obedience normally implies giving preference to the law, which the believer sees as the privileged expression of the divine will. Jesus Christ came into this dialectic of individual freedom and the commandment of authority, in order to establish or confirm a third pole of obedience: loyalty to the Spirit. This is how Paul saw it, particularly in Galations: '. . . you were called to freedom. . . . But I say, walk by the Spirit. . . . But if you are led by the Spirit you are not under the law' (Gal. 5:13-18).

Loyalty to the Spirit of Jesus which is the ultimate court of appeal both for authority and for those subordinate to it, introduces a specific dimension into Christian behaviour. In the name of acknowledgment of the Spirit, of his continually disconcerting and novel inspiration, the Christian may be called to place himself or herself beyond validly established norms. Transgression is requisite in certain circumstances, in certain stages of Christian experience, in the name of the 'Holy Spirit whom God has given to those who obey him' (Acts 5:32).

Some think that it is possible to avoid this problematical tension—which is difficult for the individual and for the established order—between responsible freedom, the safety of the norm and the demands of the Spirit, by placing these calls solely on the side of the magisterium. This demanding trilogy is thus reduced to the two familiar poles; and the authority of the magisterium is reinforced as the sole locus of expression and discernment of the Spirit. But that does not acknowledge the nature of Christian life as it is described in the New Testament and already anticipated in the Old Testament (see, *inter alia*, Numbers 11:25-9). The tension specific to Christian obedience is due to the fact that the magisterium does not have exclusive privileged access to the Spirit. Similarly, the help of the Spirit is given to the hierarchy in order that it may fulfil its specific task, but the gifts of the Spirit are in everyone (bishops, priests and lay-people) and no one is spared his disconcerting promptings.

An acknowledgment of the fact that the gifts of the Spirit aid the bishops in their work does not mean that we have to identify the Spirit with the exercise of the magisterium. Is it right to state, as did certain cardinals after the papal election: 'The Holy Spirit has chosen . . .'? Surely it is more exact to say that the cardinals, trying to attend to the promptings of the Spirit, made a choice which is nevertheless subject to human limitations? If we wholly confuse the calls of the Spirit and the decisions of the magisterium, then we remove, both from authority and from the whole body of Christians, the capacity for criticism and healthy analysis. Then creeping infallibility becomes a veritable avalanche until we assign it to all actions of the hierarchy. It was significant after the promulgation of the encyclical *Humanae vitae* that, although it was unanimously recognised as not being infallible, some people found that they could not admit that as a consequence it was fallible.

What room do we have for the charisms of the faithful if it is all taken up by the inspiration of the magisterium? There is an attentiveness to the voice of the Spirit which cannot be reduced to the task of authority and which even eludes in part the checks of the hierarchy. The prompting of the Spirit never occurs entirely within wholly authorised conditions of discernment. The faithful may be asked to move along unmarked paths, without the guarantee of the usual norms of obedience.

The Church is faced with a weighty and specific question: Either the role of the magisterium is to bring this novel ferment within the sphere of legitimate procedure, or the ecclesial community, under the guidance of the hierarchy, should be so governed that it comes to see this 'extra-institutional' presence of the Spirit as something quite normal. If that is so, the Spirit comes to render responsibility on all sides a more complicated affair. That makes for an uneasy situation as far as the extension of the gospel is concerned.

The exercise of authority is thus made the more hazardous. Some Christians (at all levels) will be worried by this. Rather than try to avoid this worry, which is inherent in the permanent entry of God into human history, it is essential to re-affirm the faith and to give confidence to the nomad people that we are. Authority cannot substitute itself for God who speaks in a cloud. If in the last analysis it is the Spirit who leads the people of God, we must make sure that it is not so restrained that only that is allowed expression which is assimilable by the powers that be, even the most benevolently established.

(*d*) Indispensable contestation

Contestation, like transgression which is its consequence, is a healthy element of a society. The Church as much as any other society cannot do without it lest its inspired creativity wither. The frequent appeal to unanimity which can even be imposed on pain of discipline is a dangerous weapon which dispenses with any welcome for divergent opinion, any distinction between the essential and the contingent, and any consideration of criticism and questions which are somewhat disturbing to the *status quo*.

D

How imprudent it is not to allow, even by institutional measure, a true right of speech to minorities which are always disturbing, to those who live through strange and novel situations, to those who try to live and express their faith in Jesus Christ within forms of modern thought. How imprudent it is to define 'Christian morality' for instance in such human experiences as sexuality when ethical conditions and implications are changing, much more by reference to former decisions than to the present-day existence of men and women of the moment. How imprudent it is to exclude women from all the organs of thought, responsibility and decision in the Church. There is a mode of comprehension which women have of the Good News—and the gospels offer enough evidence of this—that is non-reducible to masculine understanding and whose soundness and richness are essential to the community. How imprudent it is to believe that the clergy, who live even more outside the normal conditions of life as they 'rise' in the hierarchy, can validly see from within what the grass-roots faithful, who are also baptised, filled with Christ and empowered by the Spirit, feel, experience, look for and discover.

Is it true that only those who have the reins of power can effectively try to interpret and understand what Jesus wills for his Church, in particular the fullness of ministries, the according of responsibilities and the powers of authority? Surely the bishops run the risk—as a contemplative said in regard to the Council—of 'defining themselves in relation to themselves'?

Some people will find such suggestions blasphemous inasmuch as they forget that—happily—divine inspiration in the Church does not mean the cancellation of human reality within it, and that the Church has an urgent need not of the moral judgment of individuals but of a constant effort at analysis and readjustment of its institutions. What is at issue is not the value, devotion and sacrifice of those who run the Church but the adaptation of its institutional operation. Care for and commitment to the Church, whether one is a theologian, grass-roots priest or above all a member of he simple faithful, means no derogation from the Church's specific mission. Obedience in its various instances does not exist in order to assist the work of authority but to benefit the common good through the growth of community.

(e) Inward solitude

If he or she undertakes this difficult task of contestation, the Christian (whether he or she is lay-person, a priest or a bishop) to some extent experiences the solitude of Jesus. This is a solitude beyond all human guarantees. The understanding of a few friends, however reassuring it may be, does not absolve one in the last analysis from having to take the final decision alone. The conviction which spurs one to enter into conflict does not free one from hesitation and uncertainty. But it is right that things should be thus. Such doubts about oneself and about the cause which one is defending enable one to avoid fanaticism. They allow room for research, for questioning, for new elements, and for dialogue.

Because we have to follow new paths and are impelled to call in question the established order which to date has been—for the questioners too—our guideline; because we have to walk into the mist and face the unknown; and because conviction about what is no longer valid does not necessarily bring understanding of what has to be put in its place, contestation is all the more trying inasmuch as it has to do with the most basic experiences. It is hardly possible sometimes not to be tempted to believe oneself abandoned by everyone, on the Mount of Olives, where only the last spark of certain faith still gleams.

Surely every Christian is summoned sooner or later, in different ways, however, to experience this essential solitude. It is inherent in the Christian calling. The mission of the Church authorities is not to remove this insecurity from Christians. Nevertheless Church-people are constantly tempted to surrender themselves to an infallible authority which takes away from them all risk of venturing on uncharted ways. If they agree to such wishes, the hierarchy, so to speak, interpose themselves between God and his people. By trying to avoid mystery and openness, the hierarchy could eventually suppress faith: 'Blessed is the man who trusts the Lord, whose trust is the Lord' (Jer. 17:7).

*   *   *

In his private life as in his external attitudes, sometimes in the name of obedience, a Christian has to take up a position which is against or beyond even the most authorised of laws. Then he perceives an especially difficult situation without the certainty that his transgression is sufficiently under the guidance of the Spirit. Often it would be preferable to keep to the security of the norm, yet one can be called to disobedience, to the service of values that one realises are primordial and insufficiently acknowledged.

In these 'deviant' situations, prudence demands that certain criteria of discernment should be invoked. They are to be found *inter alia* down at the grass-roots, in confrontation with one's peers. Perhaps the *sensus fidei* and 'reception' by the people of God have been somewhat obscured as traditional means of verifying the discernment of the Spirit. But to reserve that discernment to authority would mean the destruction of what specifically constitues transgression.

Of course illusions and mistakes are possible. Do they have to be dramatised?

Such ambiguities are the normal condition of the people of God on their pilgrim way. It is the situation of the custodians of authority as much as of the whole company of the faithful.

'Take care what you do with these men (says Gamaliel to the High Priest and to the Council) . . . I tell you, keep away from these men and let them alone; for if this plan or this undertaking is of men, it will fail; but if it is of God, you will not be able to overthrow them. You might even be found opposing God.' (Acts 5:35, 38-39).

Translated by John Cumming

Jean-Claude Sagne

Christian Obedience and Acceptance of Death

CHRISTIAN OBEDIENCE always contains a reference to the mystery of Jesus, who 'humbled himself and became obedient unto death, even death on a cross' (Phil. 2:8). The Christian life is nothing less than the imitation of the life of Jesus, an imitation which is not a literal copy but rather a personal effort to capture the immediacy of the inspiration which guided Jesus. It is therefore essential to stress the relation between Christian obedience and the cross of Jesus in the sense that the cross of Jesus draws our present conduct towards a total abandonment to the will of the Father through our everyday life. I want to keep at the centre of these reflections a positive and stimulating conception of Jesus' obedience as a passion to discover and carry out the Father's will for his life. It is therefore essential to meditate on Jesus' obedience to the Father's will with reference to his own death before drawing conclusions from it about the nature of Christian obedience and the usual place within it of the acceptance of death.

The theme as a whole may be summed up as follows: Jesus wanted to do the Father's will even to the point of giving his whole life in obedience to that will; we, in our turn, must make our own the obedience of Jesus to the point of giving our lives when the Father's will calls on us to do so. What Jesus did we must do after him. However, there is a radical difference between Jesus' situation and our own: he obeyed because he was the Son of the Father whereas we obey him who is our Lord and our God. In other words, Jesus' obedience to the Father took place in a climate of initial familiarity of which we have no experience, except, and still only partially, through the deepening of our love for God. There cannot be too much of the action of the Holy Spirit to give us back something of the freedom of the children of God within obedience. When we are faced with accepting death the difference reappears, pregnant with consequences. Jesus was able to give his life in obedience to the Father, knowing that this supreme gesture was the climax of his existence as the Son returning to his origin and source, the bosom of the Father. For us, acceptance of death becomes really bearable only to the extent that we discover in our human condition the living trace of this gift of the Father calling us to become sons and daughters in the Son and promising us, through that filial existence, the fulfilment of our wishes, the assumption of our human endeavour into a divine future, the full realisation of our identity as creatures of desire through rest in the infinite love of the Three Persons.

This is simply another way of saying that Christian obedience can become an acceptance of death only to the extent that it is immersed in the mystery of Jesus as Son of God. The more a reading of the life and death of Jesus tends to make them resemble the courageous gift of a hero sacrificing himself for a human cause, the more imitation of Jesus moves towards a struggle against the instigators of injustice, while renunciations in our present life become detestable and unjustifiable, when indeed they are not seen as an alienation cloaked by a distorted ideal of religion. There is a choice here in Christian life and the imitation of Jesus Christ, and acceptance of death is the issue which forces it on us. The more we try to reduce the life and death of Jesus to a human venture of solidarity with the most deprived of a period, the more we make it impossible for ourselves today to understand how Jesus' obedience can be a source of life and liberty. On the other hand, a more theological reading of the life and death of Jesus as the movement of the only Son towards the Father has the perceptible consequence of a sort of transfiguration of something which previously seemed to us the ultimate in inhumanity and unacceptability, the acceptance of death. In one context acceptance of death is seen as a more or less lucid and painful resignation to the inevitable, before the frontier which cannot be crossed, the obstacle in nature reifying spirit or depriving it of support to reject nature. In the other, acceptance of death is the last word of freedom, in so far as a man succeeds in regaining control of himself as made by God and for God, destined to live with God's life, contemplating him and loving him without in any way ceasing to be able to go on searching for him, like a person who plunges into the ocean of peace, penetrating faster and faster and more and more deeply into the element which welcomes him and revitalises him.

I have indicated a schema and an area of discussion which support each other: acceptance of death in Christian obedience is human only if it is a continuation of the offering Jesus made as the final expression of his nature as Son of God and in God, a human offering, yes, but made as the final return of the Incarnate Word to the bosom of the Father who is his origin and resting place. It is time to give a more precise content to this idea by dwelling at greater length on the mystery of Jesus in which our Christian existence finds more than its meaning—its legitimation and only possibility of being lived and desired.

1. JESUS' OBEDIENCE AS A RETURN TO THE FATHER

In the life of Jesus, right from its starting point in the incarnation, there is a movement of return to the Father. The author of the epistle to the Hebrews mentions this when he attributes to Jesus 'when he came into the world' the words of Ps. 40 which reverberate as a commitment to God, a vow:

> 'Sacrifices and offerings thou hast not desired, but a body hast thou prepared for me;
> in burnt offerings and sin offerings thou hast taken no pleasure.
> Then I said, "Lo, I have come to do thy will, O God,"
> as it is written of me in the roll of the book.'
> (Heb. 10:5-7, quoting Ps. 40:6-8)

In this quotation, which is itself a commentary on and exposition of the original psalm text in Hebrew, we have a clear indication that the Son had an intention when he took flesh of our flesh: 'I have come to do thy will, O God.' As man, Jesus is defined by his obedience to the Father's will. Since the context of the psalm treats the sacrificial procedures of Levitic worship as less important than an interiorisation of obedience, Jesus' obedience is presented as going beyond and also fulfilling the sacrificial system. Nevertheless, since man has nothing better to offer than himself, if outward gestures and gifts in kind are called in question obedience can supply an ultimate proof in the sacrifice of self. It is true that giving one's life is not necessarily inspired by a giving of oneself to others; the intention of a physical action is not transparent, but everyone is well aware of the value he attaches to his own life—we do not step out of life as we take off a coat. Thus the sacrifice of his life is indeed the supreme proof of the Son's obedience in his human state. The proof is not the reality of the sacrifice, but where the sacrifice finds the place and matter of its achievement. Jesus' death is not in itself the act of his obedience to the Father's will, but it is, beyond all doubt, the condition which enabled that obedience to become actual and effective in the furthest recesses of Jesus' heart and desire as he faced life and death. A promise must be kept if it is to be completely given. Jesus made a promise when he came into the world and kept it by undergoing the torture of the cross. There are things one cannot fully give until one has tried or tasted them, rather like a person who discovers a new landscape towards which to turn his steps or again like a person who feels the awakening within himself of a new sensibility, a call to love or create. In the same way it was necessary for Jesus to taste death before he could offer himself totally to the Father.

Here again, the author of Hebrews draws our attention to the condition of the incarnate Son as a path of obedience leading finally to an acceptance of death: 'Although he was a Son, he learned obedience through what he suffered; and being made perfect he became the source of eternal salvation to all who obey him' (Heb. 5:8-9). The statement is extremely concentrated, but there are at least two things which stand out immediately: obedience brings the Son to the perfection of his existence in our flesh and in the same way Jesus' obedience opens our hearts to their salvation. To put it in different, less systematic language, Jesus had to take his obedience to the point of suffering for it in his own flesh and as a result he was brought to the fullness of his filial life as Son of God made flesh for our salvation, the saving Word. The great lesson on which the epistle to the Hebrews meditates is the assimilation of the Son of God to the humility of our condition which is revealed in the weakness and sin in our lives, the weakness of flesh which is subject to suffering and death, and the sin of the heart which disobeys the law expressing God's will.

Thus, in one way or another, Jesus' obedience is situated between a point of departure, the intention of sacrifice, and a final point, the consummation of that sacrifice on the cross. By Jesus' obedience I mean his constant disposition to seek to know and do the Father's will. St John's gospel reminds us many times that in everything Jesus acted at the Father's command, modelling himself on the Father's example and instructions (see John 5:19; 8:28-29; 12:49-50). As for Jesus' sacrifice on the cross, a matter which has once again become the subject of controversy, I shall define it, following the epistle to the Hebrews, as the sacrifice Jesus freely made of his own life to reconcile us with the Father by drawing down the Father's pardon on our sin and restoring to the Father the obedience of repentant man. Jesus lived his passion as a sacrifice by interceding as high priest for the sins of the people and replacing the old sacrificial system by the gift of his life. Here we cannot avoid saying something about the sacrificial significance of Jesus' death on the cross in obedience to the Father's will, because it is here that Christian obedience finds its basis and ultimate meaning. It is also essential to stress once again that Jesus' obedience included the resolve to prefer the Father's will to any other thing, whether it be the will of men or Jesus' own will in his humanity.

All that I have been able to say about Jesus' obedience as a man can be summed up in three short statements: Jesus always wanted what the Father wanted; he put the Father's will before his own life; he accepted death as a sacrifice of reconciliation. The fundamental point to remember from all this is that Jesus' obedience is a constant prior reference to the Father's will, something very different from conformity to a written law or to the customs of the dominant class or the example of the cultural élite of his time. It is this constant reference on the part of Jesus to his Father's will which manifested him to his contemporaries and then to us as the Son. This is very clear in St John's gospel: 'he . . . called God his own Father, making himself equal with God' (John 5:18). The context gives us clear proof that the situation was a dispute about obedience to God. Jesus had healed the paralytic at the pool of Bethzatha on the sabbath (John 5:9, 16), which the Jews felt to be a scandalous and almost provocative offence. Jesus, however, presents this healing as a work of obedience to the Father's will. In doing so he stresses the immediacy of his obedience to the Father, implying that he is in continuing personal relationship with him. Here the obedience of Jesus in his humanity is already invoking his divine nature as the Son constantly turned towards the Father, attentive to his word and his will. But this is not all. Not only does the divine status of Jesus as Word in God explain the unforced quality of his obedience to the Father, which transcends human precepts while at the same time fulfilling the Mosaic law given by God, but, even more important, the filial existence of Jesus in his humanity appears as the perfect expression of his divine nature as Son in the mystery of the exchanges between the Three Divine Persons.

2. THE LIFE OF THE SON AS A RETURN TO THE FATHER

Jesus' human obedience is the reflection and sign or again the typical result of his life as Son turned towards the Father. It is true that obedience is a human thing, implying dependence on another person who is a witness of the unity of the group around a common endeavour and guardian of a law expressing the experience acquired by those who founded and built up the group. The Word of God does not obey the Father if obedience implies the inequality of the two partners and the dependence of the subordinate on the possessor of authority. There is no need to elaborate on this point. The Son is the equal of the Father in all things. The Father communicates to the Son all that he is and all that he has. The Father keeps nothing for himself; he is the one who gives. What characterises the Father as a person is precisely his generosity: by the movement of his love, which is the gift of his divine life, he constitutes before him in that same divine existence that only Son who is 'the splendour of his glory and the expression of his being' (Heb. 1:3). The one difference is that between the source and what flows from it, the difference of origin between what gives everything and what receives everything. The Father is for ever the living source of the Son's existence, and the Son is God born of God, light born of light, true God born of true God. The Son's existence is the constant result, the end, of the Father's unceasing gift: the Son receives himself from the Father's gift. Consequently the whole life of the Son in God is a movement of return to the Father to face the one who gives him everything, who even gives him his self.

This return of the Son to the Father is in no sense a fusion which would annihilate in one denial both the gift by the origin and the receiving by the recipient. In the language of human love the dream of fusion with the loved one conceals the fear of being dependent on the other and the subtle desire to destroy him or her. In Christian spirituality the idea of fusion, where it occurs, conceals a denial of the mystery of creation and a misunderstanding of the mystery of the Trinity. The Son's return to the Father is therefore not his reabsorption into the One, wiping out the distinction between the Three Divine Persons. No, the meaning and effect of that return is the precise opposite. The Son returns to the Father, but in order to recognise him as Father by praising him for his generosity and adoring him in his divinity. I cannot help using the human language of prayer to describe the movement of the Son towards the Father, which is like the return gift in an exchange, the act by which the recipient discharges his debt of gratitude towards the giver. The return gift which establishes active reciprocity between the partners in the alliance, by so doing also differentiates them. The distinctive feature of the relation of alliance is to establish different roles between the parties to the alliance. The role of the person who took the initiative and made the gift is different from the role of the person who accepts this first gift and develops a personal response in terms of a gift returned, given back, and of gratitude shown by words of thanks and shared joy.

Much could be said about the nature of the return gift in the practice of exchanging gifts to establish an alliance as solidarity in peace. Many people regard the return gift as the disguised expression of a sort of servitude, as though the person placed under an obligation by the giver had to pay back a debt with interest. The gift in return usually provokes accusations of lies and hypocrisy; it is said to be a sort of currency dressed up as a present to deceive the supporters of freedom and spontaneity against a background of individualism and inhuman unreality. In fact the return gift is the path of creative freedom. The only person who is really free is the one who has learned from the gift of the other to give his freedom in a deed or a gesture which expresses and commits his whole self. The only person who is really free is the one who is capable of risking his freedom in a promise and capable of obedience. For the moment let us bear in mind at least that the return gift is the response to an appeal which stimulates in the person who receives it the energy to create in order to give. No one would be able to give if he had not received a gift from another which he had recognised as such and welcomed with his whole self as an invitation to give in return. The return gift is the awakening of a freedom which has been wholly constituted by the gift of the other and accepts its identity by entering into the exchange of gifts.

I would also say that the gift in return is typically the act of the son or the child recognising its father's gift. The education given by parents always devotes a lot of attention to helping the child to identify parental gifts. At table the child learns to ask for water and bread and, above all, to express gratitude: 'Say thank you.'. Parents are usually very keen on this relatively personalised expression of gratitude centred on food, which makes present and prolongs the gift of life. It would be facile to denounce this as a demand for love on the part of parents incapable of free giving. Parents attach so much importance to the child's expression of gratitude because it is a necessary step towards the gift in return. A child cannot give something to someone else unless he has learned what a gift is by meeting it in the repeated action of givers of food, which is what his parents are first, before they are the givers of the language of gratitude. It can also be easily observed at table that a child comes to share its food only to the extent that it first sees its parents take food from the dish to serve it. Only a person who has been served and has, however little, appreciated the gesture of service as a humble gift of love can put himself at the service of others in a gift which perpetuates the cycle of alternate and interdependent gifts. The return gift is thus the action of an emerging maturity, foreshadowing the generosity of the gift which does not know what response it will provoke. In fact, the gift in return is the typical act of human freedom since that freedom is always something received from the gift of others and from the gift of God. The practice of the exchange of gifts, far from being alienating, is where freedom on both sides is exercised and grows, since our freedom becomes real and active only when someone awakens it and summons it by a first gift indicating their love. The exchange of gifts makes our freedom a springboard for a sort of mutual creation with the one we love.

If I may venture to apply these ideas to the life of the Son of God, I would say that he exists only through the Father and for the Father and that he expresses his existence in a return gift which orients his whole being to praise, adoration and Eucharist. This is simply the definition of a love which knows that it has been awakened by the gift of the other and wants to reach fullness through its gift in return. It is thus possible to see in Jesus' human obedience the translation for us and the revelation in his behaviour and his words of his divine nature as the Son. This applies in a special way when Jesus' obedience reaches its culminating point in acceptance of death. Of course, Jesus offers up his life in accordance with the order he has received from the Father and, even in this sense, his obedience in the face of death rests on his relation with the Father. But that is not all. Jesus' sacrifice of his life expresses his movement of return to the Father who has given him everything. It is in the measure that he places his life in the Father's hands in total abandonment, the last word of filial trust, that Jesus can show that he is the Son: death cannot deprive him of his deepest life, even if it can deprive him for a time of his humanity. Death will open wide for him the door to life in that the deep, hidden life of Jesus is communion with the Father. The act of Jesus' death, his resolve of filial surrender summing up his whole life in a perfect, final sacrifice, places the whole of Jesus' human existence within the infinite love of the Son for the Father through the living flame of the Spirit, 'the burning seal which makes them one', as the Easter liturgy (the Toulouse hymn 'Joyous Light') puts it.

It would therefore be an impoverishment to reduce Jesus' death to a sort of heroic obedience to the order of a legitimate and accepted superior. It is much more than that. It is the sacrifice the Son makes to the Father of the humanity he has received from him, within the Son's eternal movement of return to the Father, his source and origin. The aspect of reconciliation and sacrifice adds another level to this living and unique reality. The incarnate Word's perfect obedience is a sacrifice of reconciliation precisely in leading to suffering and death under the blows of sinful men and to the choice of the Father's will before any other good, whereas man's sin from the beginning consisted in the attempt to guide his whole life instead of following the advice of God, who showed him good and evil. I shall finish on this point by noting that Jesus' death in obedience to the Father's will is nothing other than the perfect expression of sonship, characterised by trust and surrender, where man's sin was refusal of sonship in the name of a desire to live his life by his own resources, disregarding the law by which the Father was guiding his life towards happiness.

3. CHRISTIAN OBEDIENCE AS A RETURN TO THE FATHER

Christian obedience is the imitation of Jesus' obedience through complete docility to the Holy Spirit, whose inspiration enables us to follow Jesus' movement to the Father in terms of our particular vocation and in the forms of evangelical witness recommended by the Church in our time. In this connection, the most typical and complete example of Christian obedience is martyrdom, a fate very present in many countries of the world where our fellow Christians are still or again being persecuted in our own day. It is not at all surprising that the Holy Spirit should have been in the heart of Ignatius of Antioch as he went to his martyrdom, the source of living water which murmured, 'Come to the Father'. Ignatius of Antioch here expresses with particular clarity what the acceptance of death means for someone who is trying to be fully identified with the mystery of Jesus in his death through obedience to the Father's will.

I regard martyrdom as the typical and perfect act of Christian obedience, but I do not thereby mean to imply that it is a path which all can follow. Martyrdom provides a sign of what Christian obedience involves when the gift of one's life is made in the same way as Jesus', in imitation of 'the faithful witness' (Rev. 1:5) 'who in his testimony before Pontius Pilate made the good confession' (1 Tim. 6:13). Of course it is perfectly clear that not every Christian has either the material possibility or the divine call to re-enact the death of Jesus by sacrificing his life in witness to the faith. It is not given to all to undergo that trial of faith which consists in giving one's life in a single act under the blows of persecutors. Nevertheless, for every Christian martyrdom should represent, not an exceptional fate, but the manifestation in light of the desire which is written in the depths of his heart by virtue of his baptism. In remoulding us in the image of the life-giving death and resurrection of Jesus, baptism fills us with the fullness of the same Holy Spirit who led Jesus to the cross and to the Father. The epistle to the Hebrews tells us that Jesus offered himself as an unblemished victim to God 'through the eternal Spirit' (Heb. 9:14). The Spirit we received at our baptism is a Spirit of sonship in us because he comes to us from the Father through the Son and draws us to the Father through the Son. In us therefore he is a Spirit of obedience and sacrifice, a Spirit of adoration and praise, a Spirit of trust and surrender, everything which belongs to the state of sonship. In the heart of every baptised person there is a desire for the cross which is the mark of the indwelling of the Holy Spirit. The same desire in us is a desire for life through a return to the Father. In other words, Jesus' death on the cross is, both for him and for us, the only road to life, the only source of true life for us in God.

In this perspective, acceptance of death is not a particular case of Christian obedience, but much more what constitutes Christian obedience, that is, our willed and joyful participation in the mystery of Jesus in the humiliation which led him to his glorification. There is therefore no Christian life without that obedience, which becomes *real* only in acceptance of death for Jesus and like Jesus. Of course, this acceptance does not take the form of martyrdom for all or even for many, but martyrdom is nevertheless every Christian's model. In feasts of martyrs, whether close to us in history or remote, we always experience a swelling of the heart, a joy, a movement of spiritual freedom, as though a sudden illumination were reminding us of the essence of our Christian life. It is remarkable how often we find a very close presence of Jesus during the sufferings of martyrs, who converse with him joyfully, as did the little Blandine in Lyon in 177. Martyrdom is the last word of baptism as an immersion in the death of Jesus: 'Do you not know that all of us who have been baptised into Christ Jesus were baptised into his death? We were buried therefore with him by baptism into death, so that, as Christ was raised from the dead by the glory of the Father, we too might walk in newness of life' (Rom. 6:3-4). Without this acceptance of death, which is always against the background of martyrdom, the Christian passes by the mystery of his vocation as a believer and a baptised person and deprives himself of the freedom of the children of God.

Christian freedom cannot be anything other than our participation in the freedom of Jesus. Jesus displayed his freedom to the highest degree when he stood his ground and remained faithful before the Jewish chief priests and Pontius Pilate, who had on their side the violence of the crowd and of the state machine, two contrasted but complementary faces of the power of death. Acting through these men, ancient rulers or new occupiers, was also the whole culture of an epoch, a whole body of prestigious knowledge, whose internal contradictions did not prevent momentary coalitions for the sake of expediency. Jesus was free in not yielding to this human power and relying only on the Father's Word, the source of all truth and all life. Jesus' freedom is expressed in his consent to death to bear witness to the Father.

Our human freedom has no other path than that of Jesus. This is more than a psychological issue, serious though that is. The person who is afraid of death is not free. The anguish of death is the hidden source and the model of all anguish. Fear of death impedes life in the present by many, often subtle, fetters, which tend to encourage contradictory quests, from desperate attempts to keep ahead of death, repeated mad risks, to eventual apparent or real paralysis. On a purely human psychological level acceptance of death is the necessary condition for any form of creation or love, giving or fruitfulness. In this sense, therefore, life is only possible, humanly speaking, through the acceptance of death. However, the type of freedom the Christian acquires by accepting death goes much further than that wisdom of a giving which can take a risk because otherwise it would not exist. There is no giving to another which does not presuppose a relinquishing which is eventually felt as a loss. Life, too, is possible and real only when ruled by giving, which once again means by acceptance of death. It is impossible to live while wanting to hold on to one's life. The dominator, the master in Hegel's parable, the person who lives by his own resources and for himself, reducing others to slavery and treating them as passive objects of his whims, that man remains alone, delivered up to the power of death. His fear of death is expressed in his refusal to recognise the other, to love him as an equal, to expect something from him in a dependence which he eventually admits. Obedience is a school of humanity and love. And nevertheless Christian obedience also has a greater power which derives from its theologal scope.

To obey like Jesus in going to the extreme of giving one's life is to cross the boundaries of the present and of our experience and enter into the mystery of the Three Divine Persons, which is happiness and peace. Human struggles, even for the best causes, keep their militants in a constant state of insecurity and fear. Of course this may seem to encourage clarity and energy, though it may result in making the simplest things complicated and making people ignore their own lives in an extended disregard for the present in favour of an exaggerated quest for alternatives. A Utopia is in great danger of being a dead end into which men divert their hopes, making quite relative aims absolute and forgetting the end of the journey of life. Only the desire to return to the Father through obedience can give, here and now, interior unity and peace through constant active participation in the Son's eternal offering to the Father.

But what about our Christian obedience and our acceptance of death in our daily lives? All of us of course, agree here and now, to slip our deaths one day into the death of Jesus, our drop of water into the cup he was able to drink for us. One day we shall reach the end of the road, and our life as it ends will give our poor human words their meaning and reality; sincere they may be, but how subject to testing and verification. But before that there is the great simplicity of the everyday. What we must at all costs not do is imagine our participation in the cross or dream of the extraordinary. The real acceptance of death today for each of us is our disposition to do completely the will of the Father as he reveals it to us. The spiritual road open to all Christians without exception is surrender to divine providence, that is the passion to seek and do in everything the will of the Father, as Jesus did. The death to be accepted is first of all death to that in us which is an obstacle to trust in God and others, an obstacle to fraternal service and giving. That is why Jesus' obedience, by destroying in us the roots of sin and restoring to us the freedom to obey the Father totally, gives us back the freedom of the children of God, a freedom which unfolds in praise, adoration and self-offering: 'I appeal to you therefore, brethren, by the mercies of God, to present your bodies as a living sacrifice, holy and acceptable to God, which is your spiritual worship' (Rom. 12:1).

Translated by Francis McDonagh

PART III

Problems of our Time

Clodovis Boff

Towards an Ethic of Critical-Social Obedience

INTRODUCTION

OBEDIENCE to the law and, more widely, to the social order, has recently become an acute problem for many sectors of the Church. The reason for this is a growing perception of the incompatibility between the Christian faith and certain social structures. This involves theological reflection starting from the reality perceived and experienced by Christians (first section), confronting it with the great principles of faith (second section), in order to draw some practical conclusions for Christian life (third section).

In this article I propose to examine the question both from the standpoint of the relationship between ideology and politics (superstructure), and that of the economic sphere (infrastructure). The limits of this reflection are obvious: it seeks first to establish a theoretical framework, and then to set out the processes of argument by which it might be possible correctly to pose and adequately to resolve questions relating to obedience in the social sphere.

1. OBEDIENCE TO THE LAW AND THE STATE: SUPERSTRUCTURE

(a) The Data of Reality: Seeing

The legal system in a society divided into classes necessarily reflects class interests, and the interests of the ruling class will logically predominate in it. The managerial classes, acting on behalf of the ruling class, are those who use the various organs of the State apparatus, the Parliament, the Law Courts, the police, in order to maintain or increase the domination of the ruling class.

Of course, the classes confront each other within an ever-changing set of circumstances and corresponding forces, and never simply in terms of the outright domination of one class by another. In fact, society will contain laws and forces favourable to the dominated classes, but these will exist as dominated laws and forces, that is, maintained under the control of the ruling bloc. So the morality of a society in no way comprises a homogeneous whole. Equally, the dominated classes have no fixed characteristics. Through struggle, they can impose more respect for their rights and interests. This is the normal process operating in a society divided into classes.

Nevertheless, in moments of crisis, when the *status quo* of the different classes is threatened with upheaval, the ruling classes seek to guarantee their hegemony through exceptional political and legal means. So in Latin America, the capitalist classes, threatened since the mid-sixties with growing movements of popular unrest, had recourse to their military arm—the army—in order to safeguard their class interests. They therefore evolved an ideology to justify such an undertaking. This is the Doctrine of National Security, which gave birth to a whole gamut of repressive legislation.

(b) Frameworks of Faith: Judging

The traditional teaching of the Church with regard to State power has two sides: it requires obedience to the State, but within limits. These are the limits set by natural and divine laws, that is, by morality. The first expression given to them is lapidary in its simplicity: 'Render to Caesar the things that are Caesar's and to God the things that are God's' (Mark 12:17).

These two slopes of the same hill are thematically developed in Romans 13 and Revelation 13. The first refers to the authorities as 'ministers of God', attending to justice; the second describes them as ministers of the devil. The first thesis is valid as a general principle: the *truth* of authority should be respected. The second is already a critical judgment: the *reality* of power, in this case Roman forces of occupation, should be rejected. This doctrine is vigorously expressed in Acts 5:29: 'We must obey God rather than men' (see 4:19).

The concept that the authorities deserve obedience within the limits set by faith and morals has been a constant tradition in the Church, from the confessions of the early martyrs, through the Fathers such as John Crysostom and Augustine, and the Scholastics, to the more recent 'social doctrine' of the Church, as expressed first and foremost by Leo XIII, whose political teaching is fairly advanced: 'If the laws of the State are in open opposition to divine right . . . then resistance becomes a duty and obedience a crime' (*Sapientiae Christianae*, 1890). Paul VI likewise admitted the possible legitimacy of revolutionary insurrection in particular situations (*Populorum Progressio*). The unanimity and constancy of the Church in affirming the principle of obedience with reservations to the State are really quite remarkable. It should, however, be remarked that this has not lessened the contradictions in the Church's application of this principle.

Now, in the light of this firm and clear teaching, how do we judge existing political and legal systems? Surely we can say that, in so far as they enshrine the domination of one class by another, they are destitute of moral authority? And, in so far as they constitute 'institutionalised violence' (Medellín) and 'structures of sin' (*ibid.*, and see Puebla 562, 452), they are to be condemned.

This immoral character of the system can be seen most clearly at times of crisis producing military coups and the unjust legislation that follows them (see Puebla, 549). And because this legislation can only be applied through the most brutal application of force (531), it is obviously neither legal nor just. At this point, laws lose the force of law, and with it, their right to moral respect.

It should, however, be said that all this is only valid in general terms, since any political and legal system will always include some aspects of legitimacy, which will probably be independent of their class content.

(c) Lines of Conduct: Acting

Given the social conditions described above, how should Christian conscience, or rather conscientious Christians, act?

First of all, it is important to note that we are not dealing here with simply one particular law or another, but with the existing framework of law as a whole. Then, it is also a question of the political system. And here again, we are not dealing with the ethical implications of one or another directive, nor even one government as opposed to another. It is a matter of calling the nature of authority into question, which means the nature of the class which exercises that authority and its very existence as a class.

In practice this means setting the prospect of revolution, understood as a changing of the bases or structures of a society, into an ethical perspective. But this is to say all and nothing, since, as Thomas Aquinas warns in the Prologue to the *Secunda Secundae*, 'in morals, general considerations are of less use, since human actions have an individual and particular character'. Now, if the question of law and authority is a question of class, the reply to the question can only be given on the same level. So we are within the ambit of a *class morality*.

Speaking of a class morality, it is important to discount one fallacy at the outset: this expression in no way means that morality is subordinate to class interests (Lenin, Trotsky, etc.). Such a position destroys morality as such, degrading it and identifying it with mere strategy, thereby permitting the use of intrinsically wrong means, such as lies, calumny, torture, etc. Speaking of class morality implies simply that morality must take account of the class situation of an individual or a group, that is: class practices are always morally qualifiable. This, surely, is the exact opposite of the previous position? So it is not a question here of judging justice (or what is just or not) by the measure of class interests, but, on the contrary, of judging class interests (whether they are just or not) by the measure of justice. For this reason too, class morality is not and cannot be classist as such, in the sense that it can be reduced to that of one sole class—the oppressed, seen as the immaculate lamb who takes away the sin of the world. Class morality is as universal as is the proper object of morality itself: good.

Within the legal and political framework described above, each class has its social duty, or rather its 'historic mission'.

The oppressed classes, excluded from independent political participation, have the right and the duty to resistance, and even to revolution. Such a right was not originally formulated by Chairman Mao, but is enshrined in the American Declaration of Independence of 1776. It is furthermore a most ancient right, with its basis in natural law theory, and therefore considered antecedent to man-made laws. The revolutionary imperative constitutes the basic morality of the oppressed classes as such. This historical task, however, is valid only in terms of the basic commitment to an alternative social structure (the end), and in no way applies to direct strategical application (the means). The precise strategy needs to find its way, obviously in the direction of the historical project envisaged, but always in the context of existing material conditions and in the light of the corresponding ethical principles. This approach absolutely rules out the 'radicalist' ethical-political position. This is characterised by rejection of any advance within the ruling system, by the doctrine of 'the worse, the better' and the adoption of the dogmatic alternative: 'all or nothing'. Against this it should be stated that it is both possible and necessary to work within the system in order to obtain substantial advances, which will become essential steps in the great process of overthrowing the system itself. While the dominated classes continue to be dominated, their historic duty is limited to resisting domination; resisting means gaining strength—gaining strength until a radical change in the existing social order becomes possible. At this precise moment, the revolution can impose itself as the great ethical imperative. Anticipating the conditions that assure the probability of political success renders attempted revolution morally unacceptable, as *Populorum Progressio* declares.

As for the so-called 'middle classes', old and new, they too have their class morality to guide them. As far as the open and well-disposed sectors of this class are concerned,

E

there are three courses of political action they are called on to undertake:

the *critical* course, through reasoned analysis, on the part of intellectuals;
the *prophetic* course, through faith, on the part of sectors of the Church;
the *protest* course, through alternative practices, on the part of the young.

It should be said that the moral significance and political effectiveness of these courses will depend on their organic links with the process of liberation of the oppressed popular classes.

Finally, the ruling classes in their exercise of authority through use of the State apparatus: do they too have a morality within the structure here proposed? Certainly they do.

To state that the duty of the ruling classes is not to oppress, that governments should respect human rights, etc., is easy and unrealistic. As things are, the ruling classes obviously do not have the same social and therefore ethical conscience as the oppressed classes. If they had, they would not be where they are. In fact, the basic problem of a class or social morality lies not in the matter, nor the will, but in the third element of moral imputability: *conscience*. Now any basic social theory is agreed that conscience is conditioned by one's own class situation and practice, and in its turn conditions these. It is impossible for the individual to escape from this dialectical impasse, which is always shifting but also always tragic. So to expect the ruling class to possess the same moral conscience and adopt the same moral practices as the oppressed is not only contradictory but ridiculous. Only a moralising and idealist mind would be capable of imagining such a possibility. However, given that class morality does not apply to a class as a whole, but to the individuals who compose it, these always have the ethical and political possibility of operating within the room for manoeuvre that always exists in any social institution, including the State. This, however, is operating on the borderlines, and a dangerous political exercise that often ends in a moral break with the institution.

Finally, it should be recognised that in a society divided into classes, the moral practice of an individual can be very little superior to his class practice. There, duty (ethical) virtually coincides with power (political). It will be the movement of history itself, as liberator of rationality, that will create the conditions for a more advanced moral conscience and practice for all, but especially for the ruling classes.

2. OBEDIENCE IN THE ECONOMIC SPHERE: INFRASTRUCTURE

This part presupposes the argumentation put forward in the first part. It can therefore be very brief.

(a) The Data of Reality: Seeing

Obedience in the social sphere is not exhausted on the level of political relationships (with the State and its laws), but extends to the economic sphere (with the system of production). There is the world of power and there is the world of work. A moral system proportionate to its own object relates to the whole social system, that is, to the sum total of social relationships and practices, and not only to acts or some practices in the manner of traditional moral teaching.

Now, the social fabric rests on its means of production (infrastructure). These means involve social, and therefore human, relationships. And though they are established largely independently of the will and conscience of individuals, they are kept in being by individuals. So everyone in a position of authority in them is morally responsible for them, in his way and at his level.

On the economic level, the question of obedience must start from this basic premiss: the social system in which we live is based on the *exploitation* of one class by another. To fail to see the reality of exploitation is to fail to see society as it exists, and thereby to prevent oneself from setting the question of social morality in general, and of obedience in particular, in its proper context.

(b) Frameworks of Faith: Judging

In terms of a social system based, like ours, on relationships involving property, it is worth remembering that the teaching of the Church, for centuries, supported *order* in general, and defended *private property* in particular. So it was used as an ideology, in the sense of reflecting the *status quo*.

But when a realisation emerged that this order was in fact nothing more than 'established disorder' and that private property was simply the reward of rapine and theft, the teaching of the Church took another course. It still continued to defend order and property, but in a different way. It was now concerned with a true social order and with just and egalitarian distribution of property. This basic line emerges very clearly from the deliberations of the Church in Latin America, as the Puebla Documents show. There the 'extreme poverty' of this continent is condemned as 'anti-evangelical' (1159), and so is the system that produces it: *laissez-faire* capitalism (47, 64, 437, 542, 546).

(c) Lines of Conduct: Acting

In the economic sphere, individuals of different classes are called upon to fulfil a mission corresponding to their status.

The exploited must fight against the system of exploitation, within a plan of action that takes account of empirical conditions, not only for strategic or ethical reasons.

Those belonging to the middle ranks, to the extent that they recognise the movement of history and the challenges it brings, are called to take up a stance in favour of transforming the social system. Therefore, their function within the process of production should be concretely linked to the struggle of the exploited classes—the privileged agents of this transformation.

As for the capitalists, taken as a class, they evidently cannot do anything to revolutionise the system of which they are the beneficiaries. But, taken individually, they can always do something. But what? Do we need to have recourse to Marx to teach them lessons on their most elementary duties as citizens? There they would learn that their 'involuntary' function within the whole system can only be exploitationary. They would also hear, however, that as individuals, they can always do something to improve matters, as in the sphere of wages, working conditions, etc., and finally that their 'chief efficacity' is situated outside the enterprise, in public life, working, for example, for improvements in industrial legislation.

CONCLUSION

Christian obedience can never have any other proper end than hearing the Word of God and doing it. This is its first and basic objective. In this sense, obedience is a form of faith and is, therefore, theologal. Other obediences, such as social obedience, can be justified theologically only on the basis of obedience to God and to his will. Therefore, the authorities of this world, such as the legal, political and economic powers, only merit obedience to the extent that they show themselves to be mediators of God's authority. So, the ethic of obedience relates to God, and the ethic of liberation relates to men. For this very reason, the obedience of the Christian in the social sphere can never be absolute, but always relative—relative to God. It can never be blind, but always clear-sighted: this implies discerning the 'signs of the times' in so far as these are historical mediatons of the will of God. And it can only be a critical-social obedience, both in terms of theoretical analysis and in terms of ethical judgment.

Now, in a society organised on the basis of unjust relationships (classes and exploitation), obedience to God implies disobedience to men embodied in a ruling class. Christian obedience, which is always critical-social obedience, prescribes the imperative of revolution as a duty to struggle for the overthrow of social structures and the practices that govern them.

At this level, theological concern is not with an ethic of social obedience, but rather with an ethic of liberation, participation and creation. In terms of strategy, however, this ethic can require obedience to the existing order. In this case, obedience is imposed not so much as a virtue as through historical necessity, either for the sake of biological survival, or for the sake of political resistance.

In any case, critical-social obedience is obedience to the God of Moses and of Jesus Christ, to the God of the Virgin of the *Magnificat*, 'the champion of the poor and humble' (*Mar. Cult.*, 37). And the decision that Christians have always taken historically in defence of divine rights, understood as religious rights when this does not mean merely ecclesiastical rights, is today the decision that Christians are called upon to take in favour of human rights, above all those of the poor, rights that should also be seen as divine because they are based on the Creator and Father. So, when the oppressed are on trial, the Christian can and must raise the same protest as the apostles raised against the Jewish authorities: 'We must obey God rather than men'. Because the cause of the oppressed is the cause of the Crucified.

Translated by Paul Burns

Christian Duquoc

Obedience and Liberty in the Church

RECENT THEOLOGICAL events have raised the question of liberty in the Catholic Church. Two theologians, J. Pohier and H. Küng, have been punished by sanctions, and this has brought back to mind how intolerant and totalitarian the Roman Church used to be, both of old and not so long ago. In consequence, Catholics and Protestants, equally concerned that believers should have freedom of expression, have asserted that right which, in theory, is enjoyed by every citizen in a western democracy. Democratic rights make demands on the Church as regards the theory and practice of Christian obedience. We can no longer consider obedience in a purely mystical or spiritual perspective; it takes on a political dimension. With this in mind, I shall study, first, the abstract nature of spiritual obedience; secondly, I shall dwell on the judicial and political content of the act of obedience; finally, I will deal with the complex matter of ecclesial mediation in the question of obedience.

1. THE ABSTRACT NATURE OF SPIRITUAL OBEDIENCE

'We must obey God rather than men' (Acts 5:29) is the reply given by Peter and the apostles to the authorities who urge them not to talk about Jesus. The principle is clear, but remains formal as long as the intermediaries which reveal God's will are unspecified. And it is here, on the level of mediation, that disagreements arise. Given our state of flux, many of those in authority dream of being able to define God's will with certainty; many of those bound to obedience also want this. Those who obey gain the assurance that the other, by his command, is rescuing their will from its inherent deformation. Even then, they would have to be sure that it was a question of the other, and not some subtle self-assertion. At all events, laws and standards do not suffice to ensure that such an act conforms to the will of God: laws do not determine the link with their particular application; they do not therefore, except in a negative sense, determine what decision should be taken in a particular situation. They involve a risk of self-will in the passage from a universal form to the concrete decision. This is the risk that the one who obeys does not want to run. That is why many religious rules go into meticulous detail: they claim to anticipate situations, at least to encompass them, and thus to eliminate the danger of a creative decision, which is a subtle form of narcissism or of pride.

59

Furthermore, laws and standards are abstract universal concepts; it is the active subject who gives them concrete meaning. Therefore, standards and laws must, when applied to a situation, be decreed by some other subject, in order to avoid the danger of self-will. God is the foundation of the law; in this sense, it is formulated by an-Other. But God does not forge the link between law and situation; this link between the law and the particular situation is made by the one who decides. So, the advantage of the law being promulgated by another is lost, as God is not an object of experience. It is the human subject who creates a relationship between the law and the particular situation. How can the deciding subject be sure that his will is in harmony with the will of God? An authority other than that of God proves to be necessary, a figure who, in determining the link between the law and the individual case, can be considered to represent God. Superiors, those in positions of ecclesial responsibility, will serve as lieutenants of God. Thus, this Other who is the source of the law will assume concrete form in the one who represents him and who determines with authority the relationship of the law to the concrete situation. Thus, to obey would be to suspend one's judgment and one's self-will, giving oneself over to a superior who represents God's authority. By obeying, one would never be wrong, one would be sure of doing God's will, because it has been made clear by God's earthly representative. Thus, the superior does away with the disturbing gap between the abstract universal quality of the law and the particular nature of the situation. He delivers the subject from his ever-ambiguous will; he puts him on a royal path: relieved of his creative responsibility, the obedient subject works at the task of sanctification, his own and that of the Church. The dilemma 'obedience to God rather than to men' no longer presents itself: the authority representing God translates God's will into practical terms. Through the action of this authorised representation, God's will is absolved from all ambiguity.

God's will necessitates the presence of a mediator. Robert's French dictionary defines obedience as follows: 'to obey is to submit oneself to someone in such a way as to conform to what he orders or forbids'. The presence of the authority in person is well brought out here. Where God's will is concerned, the mediator, by ensuring that the law is efficacious in a particular situation, relieves the subject of any creative interpretation and of any hesitation; he does away with the formal nature of the law, he cures the illusion of self-will and brings about genuine conversion to the practical aim of the law as indicative of the divine intent. Thus, spiritual obedience or submission to an authorised superior would have the advantage of guaranteeing the truth of the action, whilst precluding anguish and interiorisation. By minimising the risk inherent in any creative act, obedience would ensure a direct relationship with God's will, because the other, the superior, is henceforth the only one with responsible authority. Thus, simple obedience should be enough.

In reality, the transfer of a law to a mediator who could state its concrete, actual implications, does not remove all danger of abstraction. It presupposes a solution to the problem of representation or of authority; the question of liberty remains to be clarified.

Such a transfer presupposes that the problem of representation has been resolved inasmuch as, by a process of hypothesis, the decision of the superior which makes the law concrete is considered to be an unambiguous manifestation of the divine will.

This conviction rests on an interpretation of authority that is at once mystical and juridical.

On the mystical level: the superior is held to be a spiritual master. He has experience of God, he does God's will as though by charisma; he is able to perceive the Spirit.

On the juridical level: in the Catholic Church, the mystical interpretation of authority is usually linked to a juridical one. It is not so much a question of a guru, nominated by virtue of his spiritual qualities, as of a superior whose authority has a juridical foundation by designation: ordination, election, nomination. The process of juridical designation marks the limits of representation: the superior reveals God's will from within a system of objective references, the rules and traditions of an Order, or the laws and traditions of the Church. The juridical delimitation of representation underlines the gap between the divine will and the personal will of the superior. Yet the logic of this representation is of a mystical nature, it is the logic of the Master. Thus, it tends to undermine the objective referents proper to the field of jurisdiction. Hence, the subjectivity of the superior usurps a privileged place in the transfer from the law to its particular situation.

Relieving oneself of the burden of creative decision in order to rely on the decision of a superior raises the question of liberty. For, indeed, does not release from the risk involved in passing from the universality of the law to the particular situation, constitute abdication of the ambiguous responsibility inherent in any act of liberty, and acceptance of external guarantees without regard for their significance? Is it not to forget that, in one's relationship to the Other, the only possible liberty is creative liberty? Thus, the ideal of security in the application of the divine will serves to hide the contingent situation of God's representative and the need to risk creativity. Described in this way, the act of obedience is abstract; only by consideration of the social and political content of the act of obedience can we integrate this act into a true relationship with the guiding authority, without concealing the fact that nothing can exempt one from making a personal decision, even though this may endanger the peace of the institution.

2. OBEDIENCE AND POLITICAL CONTENT

By political content, I mean the fact that obedience to a superior's order or interdict cannot be isolated from the social situation and organisation of a group. The chosen mediator is not protected from ignorance of God's will, because his decision is made by way of evaluations of the situation or mission of the group which he is directing. To elucidate, I will take an example from within a religious order. Hitherto, it was felt that the religious life had to be lived out in community, with the specification, 'under one roof'. The religious of the order feel that this way of life hinders their evangelical witness and presence in the world. The authorities decide to uphold this interpretation, and advise other religious to see in it a question fundamental to their religious life: the Diaspora is not a disintegration, but an opening up to the future, a sign of promise.

According to the working definition of obedience put forward in the first paragraph, a decision made by those in authority should not be open to question, it being, hypothetically, in conformity with God's will. The theoretical nature of such a hypothesis is obvious: it disregards the situation of the superior in time and place, and the fact that his elected responsibility does not do away with the contingency of his judgment. His decision is risky, it may be ideological, it may lead his order into ruin.

I will choose another example which will make the gap between the decision of the person in charge and the will of God more readily perceptible. A document issued by the Congregation for the Faith has sought to invalidate the debate on the ordination of women. It states that, because of their sex, women cannot be admitted to the priesthood in the Catholic Church. Although the scriptural arguments are acknowledged to be weak, tradition is considered to be conclusive, especially inasmuch as it would express the correct symbolism of the man-woman relationship.

Unless we allow for an act of obedience deprived of any content, it is difficult to consider the decision put forward in this document as a clear and indisputable expression of the divine will. In fact, all the arguments are open to dispute, and there is nothing which leads one to think that such a decision is irreversible.

In the examples chosen, the problem of representation poses itself, and it does so in terms of the contingent nature of the content proposed. Can one bring divine ratification to bear on a decision, to the point where the contingent factors of its content, historical, social and political, lose their ambiguity? Is it necessary for the chosen representative's decision to transform into a divine absolute something which, in itself, is wholly relative and does not necessarily produce greater liberty in the world or within the Church? Does obedience to someone in what he orders or forbids abolish the need to examine the content of a decision?

I indicated above that, in the Catholic Church, the selection of an authoritative representative was juridical, that this representative did not compel attention by virtue of an experience of nearness to God, and that the legitimacy of his representative capacity was related to a legal and social order: the aims of an Institute, the mission of the Church, previous traditions, Scripture, conciliar decrees, etc. The authority of a superior or bishop does not depend on personal inspiration: he is part of a group which is the depository of the rules that govern evaluation. Thus, the decision he arrives at is not necessarily the best; there is a risk involved, and this same risk is imported to the obedience. In theory, the decision should be a creative and responsible act if its fragility is taken into account. Whilst admitting that the superior or the ecclesial authority is God's representative, one must accept equally that he holds this responsibility within a clearly defined, circumscribed space and that, as a result, the one in authority must communicate the rational elements of his decision. These elements can be judged from within a consistent order accepted both by the one in charge and he who obeys. Even when dealing with definitions of dogma, the magisterium does not refer to mystical experiences, but to the network of a traditional and communal reading of scripture.

If this analysis is not inapposite, we must recognise that any act of disobedience to a decision made by the responsible authority does not necessarily constitute a transgression of God's will; it may be a transgression of an order or prohibition which would be disastrous for the social and evangelical task of the ecclesial group.

Because obedience is firstly of the political order and not of the mystical, transgression holds a positive place in the growth of the Church. Any group is as though instinctively and vitally concerned to maintain the balance of its forces, its expectation of survival; it strives to consolidate the laws of its existence. The orders of those in authority are characterised by this internal logic. Unfortunately, the balance of forces is not always the best way of furthering the social and historical function of a group. When challenges and threats appear, endangering the former balance of the group, the decision required to establish a new balance within the group does not emerge automatically.

The ecclesial group is not protected from the laws which regulate human groups, bearing in mind the variables inherent in their organisation and their aims. The ecclesial group has a function within history: to bear witness to Christ as the absolute destiny of humanity, and to bear witness not by way of speculation, but by the prefiguration of an ecclesial life of fellowship. In between this requirement and the actual situation, various intermediary factors come into play: first, the evaluation of those elements in the world which anticipate the gospel; secondly, the weighing up of the good and bad aspects of the group's own traditions, and of the changes to be wrought there; thirdly and lastly, the detection of fundamental points in the gospel which might be construed as threats to the stability of the group.

To illustrate the matter in more concrete fashion, I shall choose a subject which is much discussed in the Church today: ministry

Because of the shortage of priests, the Catholic Church is coming up against a situation which is inconsistent with its function as an institution. On the one hand, the Church holds that every Christian community with a social dimension has an inalienable right to eucharistic celebration. By a community with a social dimension, I mean any local community where God's word may be read and meditated on, where fellowship is possible; such a community moves towards a sharing in the Eucharist in order to bring its evangelical witness to perfection.

On the other hand, because of a secular tradition, the Church places such conditions on those who preside at the Eucharist, that those who should assume this task are in short supply. The ecclesial group is moving towards a situation where the local communities will be without official leaders and presidents who can celebrate the Eucharist. An itinerant minister, with no roots in the community, will celebrate the Eucharist from time to time. The divide between actual, local leadership and presidence at the Eucharist is opening up now: there is a change of direction leading to, on the one hand, the existence of communities which have no access to the Eucharist, and, on the other, a body of ecclesiastical officials who specialise in celebrating the Eucharist.

This paradoxical situation is not a consequence of the essential character of the ministry. In the ancient Church it could never have arisen, for she never conceived of a living local community without its effective right to the Eucharist. This privation can obtain from now on because the present system of ministry is related to a notion dependent on historical phenomena and needs, and not on the demands of the present state of Christian communities. The current system lays down as the essential character of ministry something which is no longer appropriate. As the clergy get older, the contradiction between an antiquated system and due claims appears more and more intolerable. Fruitless appeals to be admitted to the priesthood from those excluded on secular grounds do not testify to a disaffection for the faith or for the Church; the fact that these appeals are fruitless underlines the inadequacy of the proposal, having regard to the real requirements of Christian communities.

Faced with this contradiction, it seems to me that there are two possible responses: mystical or political.

The mystical response: those problems which can be pinpointed are ignored, whilst the present systematisation of the ministry is considered to be unalterable and the resolution of contradictions arising from that system possible only through a renewal of faith. In this sense, the contradictions are held to be temporary. As long as Christians remain faithful to prayer and to the Spirit, God will send workers to his Church. God's will is thus unequivocally written into the present systematic definition of ministry: male, celibate, sent to a particular local community from outside, saddled with an onerous training. The drama, if there is any, arises out of a show of indifference to such appeals on the part of the hierarchy. The ecclesial body cannot be held responsible for the present setback, which is due to the effects of secularisation or of a decline of interest in the faith. The present return to spirituality is already beginning to remove certain traits of a development which would have been disastrous for the Church had it continued at this pace.

The political response: the present inadequacy of the priesthood with regard to the ministerial requirements of Christian communities is not a consequence of the essential character of the ministry, but of the transformation of one of its historical forms, that is to say, of one of its contingent realisations, into an absolute. The fact that this form has been maintained, despite the dramatic consequencs it gives rise to, can be attributed to an inability to conceive of the ecclesial group as having a certain fluidity in its law and organisation, that is to say, with regard to its very contingency as a provisional institution and thus ceaselessly open to reform. This inability to allow for any change results from the fact that the leaders of the priesthood in its present form have narrowed their viewpoint to concentrate on their own heritage and their own interests, a move damaging both to the vitality of the ecclesial group and to the future of the ministry itself. This fact, an ecclesial requirement, is forgotten, because of the dominance of a group which claims to be the only orthodox representative of divine laws. The historical evolution of the group of believers and that of its guiding authorities have not followed the same course. The guiding group thinks it knows what is best for the future of the Church, because it considers itself to be the authorised witness to the gospel, and thus thinks that it has the privilege of help from the Holy Spirit. In reality, the Church must be thought of in its totality; it does not have a vanguard, the hierarchy, which could act as its conscience, in the same way that the Communist Party claims to be the vanguard of the proletariat. Such a standpoint would be wholly contrary to the most specific texts of Vatican II. Considered as a totality, effective as a community on a local level, the Church must give itself the means of fulfilling its mission. That is precisely what she is no longer managing to do as regards the priesthood. If alternatives to the present situation present themselves, it is because of the contradictions which result from the institutional system of the priesthood. These alternatives are sought and devised, in objective transgression of the law, in the midst of groups or communities which the guiding authority leaves to exist without the possibility, in human terms, of resolving the contradiction between their evangelical dynamism and eucharistic privation. The presence of alternatives proves that the Church is not simply a mystical assembly, but that she has a political system of organisation, interwoven with conflicting movements and interests, with differences of opinion, because of the continual flux of new or uncharted situations which must be faced clear-sightedly.

It is clear that obedience will be differently understood and practised, according to whether one favours the mystical pole, or whether one considers the political pole to be decisive.

In the first case, any transgression or illegal act will be seen to constitute a break with the divine will; in the second, the possibility of this transgression being a call of the Spirit to a different future for the Church will not be discounted. To protest against the present law, the harmful effects of which are obvious to all, in that it prevents communities from living to the full the life to which they are entitled, would open up a new field for free responsibility within the Church. To go beyond the bounds of legality may be a higher form of acknowledging God. Is that not a dangerous rejection of ecclesial mediation, as signified by her magisterial and pastoral authorities? Can one treat the Church as a political body, to which obedience is conditional and provisional? It is this which we have still to make clear.

3. ECCLESIAL MEDIATION AND OBEDIENCE

The Church is not simply a sociological group with a circumscribed, temporal goal. It is the place where the working of the Holy Spirit is symbolised in the sacraments and experienced in fellowship. This does not make the Church any less a structured group, within which varying tasks instigated by that same Spirit work together to ensure the evangelical harmony and effectiveness of the whole. Of these tasks, two have shown themselves, in history, to be very important, that of the bishops who lead communities, and that of the Church at Rome, in the person of her bishop, the pope. The bishops or the pope, chosen to rule the Church evangelically, have received the Spirit so that they might carry out their ministry justly and audaciously. The Spirit they have received is no different from the Spirit given to the whole Church.

Thus, one could maintain correctly that the Church, with her structural framework of different tasks, all of them motivated by an identical Spirit, lives out obedience in a mystical sense, Christian liberty consisting of a renunciation of self-interest in order to work without reservation for the growth of the Church. Does not the Church's mediation as the Body of Christ, given life by the Spirit, make the pursuit of guarantees for individual liberty within the Church in the face of an abuse of power by those in authority a vain quest?

That would be to yield again to the temptations of idealism: obedience and liberty in the Catholic Church can no more be identified with one another than can God's authority and that of the bishops. There exists a gap which cannot be avoided, and it is necessary for the welfare of the Church that she should cope with that gap and not abolish it as though we were already in the kingdom. To cope with that gap is to acknowledge the political dimension of the Church. It is within that space that the act of obedience, like that of liberty, will be an act of conversion.

For it is indeed when it is first assessed in terms of a political confrontation that obedience presents itself as conversion, the lucid and rational renunciation of one's own viewpoint in order to appropriate that of another. Conversion demands, on the one hand, that the viewpoint of the other should not be undervalued *a priori*, and, on the other hand, should it not be overvalued.

It is undervalued if the figure of the other, as a leader, is reduced, whether to a thirst for power or strength, or to a node of contradictory forces. The other is judged according to his true merit if he benefits *a priori* from the opinion that his viewpoint is freely adopted and responsible, and that his arguments are both communicable and negotiable.

It is overestimated when the gap between the figure of God and that of his chosen representative is no longer discernible. The consequence of this will be that decisions will no longer be negotiable; arguments become mystical, and their strength is held to derive from the quasi-divine situation of the representative. In this case, it is no longer a matter of conversion, a free adoption of another's viewpoint, but of submission. The act of obedience does not demand the sacrifice of reason nor the renunciation of the consistency of faith; it requires the renunciation of interests which are primarily narcissistic, even if they are collective. Thus, for the act of obedience to be an act of conversion, the content of the leader's decision must be amenable to communication, discussion and negotiation.

This model of negotiation, in which the word of the authorities is interpreted as a decision which has been arrived at by discussion and reasoning, seems to me reconcilable with the mediation of the Catholic Church. The Church is a group of free believers with a common end: to ensure fellowship within the community in anticipation of the kingdom, and to witness to the gospel as a matter of pressing importance for the future of the world.

That the Church is a society of free believers is due to the One in whom she believes: Jesus, the Christ. The Church confesses that Christ makes us free. This freedom is not hidden in interiorisation, but affects the whole man. Thus, it can prove itself in a social context; it finds expression in the relationships between believers and their leaders. Liberty articulates itself in terms of a law which expresses it, whilst at the same time making demands on it. By law, I mean here the collective and collegial effort to express objectively the play of a form of coexistence, defined by a common end, within a spatial dimension, where the means of pursuing this end, means determined by a variety and variation of conditions, are constantly subject to differing interpretations, and thus, to negotiations. The aim of this law is to guarantee the rules of negotiation, that is to say, to guarantee for every believer his freedom as a man. This is not an anarchical freedom, it is limited by the coexistence accepted with a view to a common end on the horizon. If this liberty is guaranteed legally and lived out in practice, obedience can be an act of conversion.

This guaranteed negotiation covers all the interests of the Church. There is no ecclesial reality which is excluded. Thus, on the highest level, negotiation has to do with the regulation of faith. In saying 'regulation', one means a consensus bringing men together as a Church. This consensus is based on the unconditional gift of oneself to Jesus. The acts and words of this Jesus are related in the gospels. The consensus symbolises the acceptance of this account as of vital importance for oneself and for the world. But this consensus does not abolish the multiplicity of interpretations, as the account remains unfinished. These multiple interpretations are the basis for the various types of relationship with God, in history and in the Church, that exist in practice. Yet these interpretations and, by way of them, the account, are put to the test by the challenges presented to Christianity amongst those cultures in which it finds realisation. These challenges can strike at its vital forces, at its fidelity, its future. They affect all believers, since a challenge always presupposes some connivance, if not complicity, and so overcoming them is not a matter of a simple authoritative, external decision. That was never the case historically, despite what an abstract history of the conciliar texts might give one to understand. Decisions reach maturity in debate amongst believers. Obviously, the forms and debates of negotiaton cannot be the same in a feudal system and in a western democracy. But interaction between the believers and their leaders is always necessary, because faith belongs to all and is not the property of the representatives. If, today, the taking of sanctions, without ecclesial debate, causes a scandal, it is because the way in which these matters are regulated has become outdated and does more harm to the ecclesial consensus than hazardous opinions. This regulation must be rethought on the basis of possible forms of negotiation. Obedience will then be a free act and not a servile one.

What is valid on the highest level is evidently valid for the practical and pastoral concerns of every day. Ecclesial law must be such that the believers are not deprived of words, nor of effectiveness: in short, power must not rest exclusively in the hands of a cast or of experts. If there is a solely vertical relationship within the Church, obedience loses its human significance, because it no longer has any negotiable content.

Obedience and liberty do not contradict one another, as long as the Church accepts that it is a group defined by a law. In this sense, the problem of obedience is, before being spiritual, a political one. To displace it on to a primarily mystical or moral axis has been one of the most skilfully perfected means by which to keep believers in a state of submission, of bondage of thought; it has deprived them of that right which the gospel recognised as theirs, the right to be the friends of God in his house and slaves no longer. In this instance, well-meaning words are of no use: it is the social dynamism of a group and the practice of its law, which are proof of its intention and its goal.

Translated by Christine Halek

PART IV

Bulletin

Carlos Palacio

A Comparative Study of the Treatment of Jesus' Obedience in some Modern Christologies

1. SETTING THE SCENE:
IS OBEDIENCE A CHRISTOLOGICAL CONCEPT?

JESUS' OBEDIENCE is a minor, even marginal theme in modern Christologies. In general—to degrees that will become apparent in dealing with each of the authors studied[1]—it is seldom an object of *explicit* study, and when it appears, it cannot be said to occupy a place in the forefront of the whole.

This fact is significant in itself. The 'marginality' of obedience in relation to Christology could be a symptom of the erratic nature of Christology in relation to theology. In any case, the fact itself is significant for the present study. In the first place, it makes it impossible to approach the subject *directly*; the thought of the different authors on the subject has to be reconstructed from elements scattered throughout their work. In the second, the scant attention paid to Jesus' obedience in modern Christology shows how far the concept has lost the primarily Christological and theological content it possessed in the New Testament, to the point where it has become insignificant for Christology today.[2]

One of the many reasons for this is worth pointing out now: we are faced with an example of the break with what might be called 'total Christology' or Christology of the totality of the mystery of Jesus of Nazareth in relation to the God he called Father. Obedience is, in effect, part of what tradition—patristic tradition in particular—called the 'mysteries' of the life of Jesus, in strict continuity with the type of theological reflection that gave rise to the 'gospel' as a new literary genre within the early community: the conviction that revelation of the saving plan of God (*mysterion* in the Pauline sense) took place *within* the totality of the life of Jesus and *through* his humanity.

It is not possible to follow here the varied course of a history that finished in the break with this overall, unitary view of the mystery of Jesus Christ. What is certain is that as the 'mysteries' of the life of Jesus were progressively exiled from Christology, the distance between what St Thomas called '*speculative* Christology' and '*concrete* Christology' increased through its own growing momentum. What was still coexistence for St Thomas, became a growing separation in the following centuries till a breaking-point was reached. Christology became increasingly a type of systematic speculation based on new concepts, foreign to the theo-logical tradition and on the margins of the specific history of Jesus of Nazareth. For their part, the 'mysteries' were literally abandoned to popular piety, stripped of authority and judgment, to the detriment of that piety (which is not always the same as the '*sensus fidei*' of the people of God) and of true Christology (which does not necessarily dwell in the speculations of specialists).

So it is not surprising that the theological importance of obedience as a properly *Christological* concept should have gradually vanished, leaving its aspect of *moral virtue* in virtually sole possession.[3] The logic of this inversion is perfect. Obedience is theologically significant only within the unitary view of tradition; separated from the totality of the mystery represented by the history of Jesus, it no longer has any revelatory nor Christological significance. Its interest lies at best in being an 'example' or model of morality. Its destiny was to lie in being directed into the ascetic-religious tradition, as its later evolution confirmed. Theological study of obedience is still showing traces of this development, with inevitable consequences for the question of Jesus' obedience and its place in Christology.

2. THEOLOGY AND TYPOLOGIES OF OBEDIENCE IN SOME MODERN CHRISTOLOGIES

To have recovered the history of Jesus for Christology is undoubtedly one of the great achievements of modern theology. The methods of historical criticism applied to the life of Jesus opened the way for important themes to find their way back into Christology, the nature of obedience in Jesus among them. So there is a certain inevitable convergence between the several authors' approach to the subject: all are obliged to follow the road of historical criticism, even if only to pass judgment on it and open up other paths. At the risk of simplifying, but with the advantage of clarifying the similarities between various approaches, I propose to take three different approaches to Jesus' obedience. The first can be described as 'exegetic-systematic reading of the history of Jesus', and is found in the work of Walter Pannenberg; the second will be called 'an approach to the history of Jesus from the concerns and priorities of the Christian communities', and its main exponents are J. I. González Faus, Leonardo Boff, Jon Sobrino and Christian Duquoc; the third approach is that of Hans Urs von Balthasar, a 'theological-spiritual reading of the New Testament as a whole'. Each of these approaches produces different typologies of Jesus' obedience.

(a) Exegetic-systematic Reading of the History of Jesus

This reading readily accepts the challenge posed to Christology by historical criticism and investigation, while rigorously and coherently thinking through the (epistemological and methodological) theo-logical implications of the process. This is the route taken by Pannenberg: a patient, passionate and responsible attempt to articulate the *concept* (and the experience) of *God* and *revelation* from the standpoint of its *historical* manifestation in the man Jesus of Nazareth.

The principle underlying his Christology is the clearest expression of what is meant by this exegetic-systematic reading of the history of Jesus: 'if Christology has to begin with the man Jesus, the question it must pose first is that of his unity with God'.[4] So, despite being one of those who have done most to invert the starting-points of Christology, Pannenberg does not start with a description of the man Jesus, but with a theo-logical interpretation of the historical relationship between Jesus of Nazareth and

God, which he sees as manifested and confirmed as *unity* by virtue of the resurrection, and the basis for recognising his divine sonship. In this way Christology and Trinity combine, and this combination is the basis for understanding Jesus' obedience as a Christological concept.

In this Christology, obedience certainly appears as one of the characteristics of the earthly Jesus (pp. 199-206), but not in the meaning given to these characteristics in so-called 'indirect' Christology, where such 'indices', separated from the overall personality and destiny of Jesus, are moralised and finally lose any Christological significance (pp. 61, 202; cf 47-61). It is not a question of a moral attitude; obedience is an all-embracing concept, with a double function: noetic and ontological. Noetic, in the first place, because it allows us to understand the *historical relationship* between Jesus and God, from the progressive understanding Jesus acquires of his relationship to the *kingdom* and of the definitive *nearness* of God (pp. 342ff). Obedience then becomes Jesus' exclusive dedication to his mission, to the service of the kingdom. This is being totally committed to the Father, an active and dynamic attitude of openness, trust, abandonment, quest for his will. Precisely because the present and future of the kingdom are not confused, Jesus can live totally dedicated to it (p. 384), even in the abandonment of not-knowing, which thereby becomes the best expression of Jesus' openness to the greater God and to his future, an ad-vent beyond his control. 'This ignorance', Pannenberg says, 'is precisely the condition for the unity of Jesus with God' (p. 345, see n. 24 on p. 344).

We can come to understand the historical relationship between Jesus and the Father by the fact that Jesus, in his consciousness of mission, lived inseparably in *unity* with God as Father and in *distinction* and absolute dependence in relation to the Logos. This is where the second function attributed earlier to the concept of obedience—the ontological—comes in. Through it, we try to express the way in which this historical relationship (of unity and distinction) is something constitutive of God himself. The human act of giving himself entirely to the Father (through his mission of service to the kingdom) is the *mediation* of his *union* with God. This is how his relationship to the Father appears in Jesus' own consciousness, and it is through this mediation that we are enabled to understand his *ontological dependence* in relation to the Logos. This is how the Son is (p. 347). If Jesus understands himself as 'He-who-stands-facing' (*Gegenuber*) God, we cannot understand his history and person apart from God. But the *distinction* Jesus introduces between himself and God is as original as the *unity* between them. He does this by calling him Father (pp. 159 and 173, n. 134). 'Jesus is the revealer of the divinity of God and an inseparable part of his being, because he is the one who obeys him in everything' (p. 347; cf 302-304 and 262). 'Obedience' was the word chosen by the early community (Heb. 5:8; Rom. 5:19; Phil. 2:8) to describe the life and work of Jesus in its totality, and to express and sum up the Son-Father relationship as constitutive of the very essence of God (p. 159).

(b) The Approach to the History of Jesus through the Christian Communities

This new type of approach was described above as a recovery of the life of the earthly Jesus through reflection based on the starting-point of the historical and social situation of the Christian communities.[5] There are two differences between this approach and the previous one. The first is the *situation* in which Christology places itself; the key to its reading is not so much a scientific preoccupation with the 'historical Jesus' as the definite choice to read the gospels and interpret them from the expectations, concerns and hopes of the Christian communities. The second is the relegation of the *epistemological and methodological presuppositions* of established theological discourse to a secondary plane. This relegaton, however, should not be understood as contempt for study and

F

thought, but as a quest for a new articulation of theological epistemology and method.

In this approach, it is normal for Christology to become more general and descriptive, with Jesus considered first and foremost as protagonist for the kingdom (*Cristología*, pp. 78-89), and with special emphasis being placed on significant concepts such as progressive understanding, liberty, commitment, conflict, etc. (*Esquisse*, p. 18f). This is undoubtedly where the riches and originality of this second approach lie: in seeing not only the relationship of Jesus to the Father, but the actual history of this relationship, from which there emerges a figure of a 'militant' Jesus, stimulating and inspiring for Christian militants.

How does the obedience of Jesus fit into this type of approach? The answer needs careful consideration. At first sight, the primacy given to *active* values (autonomy, liberty, decision, risk-taking, etc.) in the description of Jesus' historical purpose (*Paixão*, p. 22) does not fit very well with a type of experience such as obedience, with suggests *passivity* and usually refers to moral attitudes (submission, rules . . . see *Jesus Cristo*, p. 105f). Jesus' obedience, however, is not ruled out, though it is approached in an *indirect* manner: the central reference-point of Jesus' struggle for the kingdom, the Father, emerges from his unconditional devotion to the kingdom, in his trust, in his self-abandonment even unto death (*Jesus Cristo*, p. 106; *Paixão*, p. 37f; *Cristología*, pp. 79, 131). So obedience is one of the manifestations of Jesus' consciousness of his relationship and sonship, and the historical expression—on the level of human attitudes and behaviour—of what is meant by living for the mission received from his Father (*Cristología*, pp. 63-66). In this sense, obedience as a Christological concept would be rediscovered through its relation to the faith of Jesus, which, in its conflict with surrounding reality, becomes fidelity and trust (pp. 73f, 82ff, 88f).

Sobrino has developed this theme of the faith of Jesus most fully particularly in one of his finest chapters (pp. 67-94). But it is undoubtedly González Faus who provides most elements for working out the theological implications of obedience as a christological concept, if it is to be seen as illustrating the historical relationship between Jesus and God. Nor is it by chance that he is the only one who devotes a whole, though brief chapter to the subject (*Acceso*, pp. 69-74). From Jesus' historical relationship with God (experience of the *Abba* and mission of service to the kingdom: pp. 46-56; see *Humanidad* I, pp. 114-120), obedience appears as openness, active availability, a passionate quest for the will of the Father, but for a will that has to be found in the tension between his innermost consciousness (*Abba*-kingdom) and the harshness of reality (*Acceso*, p. 44). This is why it is obedience put to the final test of fidelity, obedient even unto death (p. 103). Basically, the attitude described as 'availability' is the very being of Jesus as Son, that is, a being totally referred to his Father. Mission, trust, obedience and the being of Jesus coincide in the identity of being-of-God and being-for-God. The mystery of this identity finds its unity in the consciousness of Jesus: of being man and, despite everything, not ending in himself, but in God-as-his-Father (*Humanidad* I, p. 119); this consciousness of the 'welcoming paternity of God' (*Acceso*, p. 97) is felt as radical *unity* with God and at the same time and inseparably as *distinction* from him. It is a consciousness of his *sonship*: of his purely relative being and total submission (*Acceso*, p. 49, n. 1; *Humanidad* I, pp. 360-364), to the point of recognising God absolutely, even when forsaken, and thereby meriting the title of 'obedient' (*Acceso*, p. 168). Faus succeeds in this way in expressing the unique and unrepeatable nature of Jesus' being and experience, at the same time as making them coincide with his mission: it is a matter of something that has to be *communicated* (*Acceso*, p. 49).

(c) Theological-spiritual Reading of the New Testament as a Whole

There is still the third way or typology of obedience, as represented in the work of Hans Urs von Balthasar.[6] If we call this third reading a 'meditation', this will serve to indicate both the author's originality and theological bent, as well as his reservations with regard to the method of historical criticism as a way of approaching the New Testament and extracting the figure of Jesus from it. Von Balthasar's constant concern is to protect the unity and totality of the 'image' of revelation. This is what the very presuppositions of the historical critical method will never allow it to do. If it forgets its own (necessary) limitations and claims to be the only 'scientific' means of approach to Jesus, it becomes blind, incapable of seeing—as contemplative faith can—the 'objective image' of revelation.

In von Balthasar's Christology, obedience is undoubtedly a totalising concept, the theological density of which requires unravelling from both Christological and anthropological standpoints. From the Christological point of view, Jesus' obedience, as Son, combines the *act of receiving* his being uninterruptedly from the Father (downward movement: the One Sent, mission) and the *act of giving himself* and responding without reservation (upward movement: availability, human execution). From the anthropological point of view, the inseparability of the divine and the human in Jesus Christ confers such a weight on anthropology that man and history can only be thought of from Jesus Christ (not from an empty transcendental structure) as the grammar and expression of God himself. In this way, obedience is not only the key to reading the whole historical existence of Jesus, but the constituent synthesis of his being, the centre towards which his human and divine dimensions converge, and in which they meet.

The heart of his obedience will only become clear 'from above', starting from the Incarnation (mission), that is, from the depths of the mystery of the Trinity. This is what von Balthasar calls the 'transcendental' or '*a priori*' dimension of Christ's obedience. *Ob-audire*, in the literal sense, is the translation into existential terms of intra-trinitarian ontological dependence, of the act by which the Son receives his being continually from the love of the Father (*PuI*, p. 135 and n. 2). If the divine process of 'procession' can be called obedience, this is because the Son, by the very act of receiving his *being*, also receives the *will* of the Father, and *assents* to it as to his own (*ThG*, p. 24f).

The other dimension of obedience, its 'conceptual', human-existential dimension, is the absolute and unconditional response of the man Jesus to the mission he receives from the Father. This intra-divine dependence can only be expressed in human language as willingness to the point of his own ruination. This language starts not as an expression of violence but one of love, not as a word spoken by chance, but out of obedience (*H*. I, p. 456f; *MySal* pp. 195f; 207ff). So, in speaking of the Word made flesh, one almost has to say that the 'form' of his obedience has to be kenotic to express this dependence. But von Balthasar not only cannot imagine the descending movement in Jesus separated from the ascending, but he can only see them both from above, that is, as an event whose *subject* is God and which *therefore* concerns man in his relationship to God (*H*. I, pp. 454ff, 459f). When Jesus takes on something divine, when he 'becomes' God—this is when he appears most deeply as the Obedient Son: because the man who obeys in 'becoming' God is a God who obeys in becoming man (*H*. I, pp. 460ff; see cf. *PuI*, p. 137f; *GimF*, 89f; *ThG*, pp. 24f, 44f).

This is the key for interpreting the whole of Jesus' earthly life and the meaning of his humanity. Also, inseparably, the key to a radically conceived anthropology based on Jesus Christ, which enables us, first, to understand the historicity of Jesus, the unfolding of the 'figure' in the 'mysteries' of his life on earth: this is the plane on which his obedience lies. Time is the setting for the response, not as disposal of self (autonomy), but as total dedication to the mission received (heteronomy); the refusal to determine his history for himself, so as to allow himself to be led by the Spirit. True freedom originates in listening (*Erhorchen*) and becomes freedom in obeying (*Gehorchen*) (*GimF*, p. 256). For Jesus, having time, *real time*, means having time for God (*H*. III/2.

pp. 150-161; *ThG*, pp. 31-39).

Second, it enables us to see the man as constituent openness and availability to God or as the language and expression of God. By addressing himself to the world, by projecting himself outward as Christ, this Word of God reaches to the very structure of our being (*H*. I, p. 459f), forms us in advance (pro-poses) as being who seek and ask till they find the res-ponse, that is, till they understand themselves as 'existing in receptivity' (*ThG*, pp. 23-31). This is the philosophical-anthropological root of obedience, or what might be called man's 'responsorial structure': he is a hearer (*Hörer*) and therefore obedient (*Gehorchen*). This can only be understood on the basis of the indissoluble unity that is Christ: expression (*Ausdruck*) and figure (*Gestalt*) of the act by which God says *himself* (*redet*) by addressing himself (*anredet*) to the world. So the 'figure' of the humanity of Christ can only be 'seen' theologically, that is, from within, from his perfect submission to God (*H*. I, pp. 175, 456f; *H*. II, pp. 267-360).

3. CRITICAL APPROACH AND THEOLOGICAL CONSEQUENCES

From now on, and by way of conclusion, we can reflect on the possible relationship between the need for a more rigorous Christological elaboration of Jesus' obedience and some more present theological problems. It would, however, seem necessary first to map out a frame of reference from the New Testament.

(a) Recourse to the New Testament

The New Testament has much to say on the subject of obedience. The technical term, used most by Paul, is *hypakoê*, which clearly has a mainly theological meaning. This is also confirmed—still on the linguistic plane—by the frequent association between obedience and two other terms used in the New Testament: the 'will' of God (*thélēma*) and the 'hour' of the Father (*hôra*). So that, bearing in mind what the New Testament has to say about the existence of Jesus on earth, obedience is not just an attitude of mind like any other, but a *mode of being* that characterised the historical relationship of a man (Jesus) with God (the Father), and that on this basis also enables us to characterise Christian being as the 'obedience' that is faith (Rom. 1:5; 16:26), in the sense that this is the deepest and most constitutive relationship *of man to God*. So the New Testament would give a three-fold description of Jesus' obedience: in the first place, it is the mode of being characteristic of his *earthly life* (Heb. 5:77ff; Phil. 2:8; Heb. 10:7); in the second, it denotes Jesus' intrinsic and total *reference to God*, to the extent of not being able to live or understand himself except standing before the Father; finally, it delineates the unique and unrepeatable character of *Jesus' way*: leading in faith and bringing it to perfection (Heb. 12:2), the principle and source of all salvation (5:9; see 10:10, 14; 12:1-2), for those who obey him. But our word 'obedience' today, thanks to its historical associations with authority and the juridical order, is incapable of bearing this weight of meaning.

(b) The Meaning and Limits of the Typologies Examined

A comparison of the writers examined with the overall view of obedience provided by the New Testament permits the statement that: (*a*) each stresses *one* aspect of what in the New Testament is the whole; (*b*) tensions arise from considering different aspects as mutually exclusive dimensions; (*c*) all our writers are forced to tackle the crucial problem of the relationship between history and God. Behind these problems, it does not need too much acumen to see, lie the great tensions in Christology.

(i) The first typology

Pannenberg moves from the person and mystery of Jesus in his relationship to God (Christology) to his universal significance for history (soteriology). He has undoubtedly made the deepest and most rigorous effort at thinking out the relationship of the historical man Jesus of Nazareth with God. His method of doing so is the *punctum dolens* of all Christology, since no approach, whether 'from above' or 'from below', can presuppose or start from an idea of God that does not originate in Jesus. To escape from this strait—common to both methods—we need to interpret the history of Jesus as a case that is certainly unique and unrepeatable, but also as one that reveals a real, constitutive relationship (being free) between God and history. Obedience, as a relationship lived by Jesus with God-the-Father (Christology), is a 'mode of being', a constitutive dimension of being man (anthropology), which introduces us into the very being of God (trinitarian theology).

From this point of view, one of Pannenberg's richest contributions is his recourse to Hegel in order to broaden the concept of *person* used in theology. If the essence of the person is the overcoming of isolation through self-giving, and thus, in reciprocal and unreserved giving, communion in being (pp. 183-185; cf 347, 351-353), then, paradoxically, personhood is acquired by losing oneself in the Other so as to receive oneself totally from him (p. 347); liberty is not independence, but unity with God (pp. 362-364). Surely this is the anthropology underlying a theology of obedience in which man is originally constituted as 'hearer'? Pannenberg does not stress this *relationship of origin* sufficiently. Is there not a danger, in emphasising the future of history (eschatology as confirmation), of forgetting that the hope of history—despite its negativity, which is also somewhat diluted in Pannenberg's Christology—is based on the *originating Word* which addresses us with love (creation)?

(ii) The second typology

These writers tread the opposite path from Pannenberg: using the needs of actual communities (soteriology—the present meaning of Christ) to build up a meaningful figure of Christ. Their concern is correct and justified. There can be no Christology without community, no real approach to Jesus outside the communities that confess him. Difficulties arise when one tries to produce a coherent link—in the discipline of thought and the commitment of praxis—between the present historical existence of the community and the unique event of Jesus of Nazareth. If the figure of Jesus is to be meaningful for human history—and not only from the exemplary and ethical point of view (Jesus' 'cause')—it must be so without losing anything of its original and unrepeatable particularity.

An example of these difficulties is our way of thinking about and experiencing the relationship between God and history. Expressions like 'obeying God in history', 'human history as the history of God', etc., will only cease being the impotent desires of a pious moralism when their Christological conditions have been made clear: the humiliated presence of God in history, leaving history its autonomy and becoming silent solidarity with it. A Christology incapable of thinking through to its final consequences what the fact of having to measure ourselves against the particular, limited event of the history of Jesus (the definitive history of God with mankind) means for the building-up of history, will navigate hesitantly between two reefs: nostalgia for a Jewish-style messianism, and the promethean voluntarism of a historical moralism. The first dreams of a Messiah who never comes and of an eschatology which never comes to pass. The temptation of the second is to reduce history to ethics, as though it were possible simply to transpose anticipation of the end in Jesus Christ into the opaque harshness of history: a double nostalgia, that of 'what is to be done' (Sollen) and that of the 'new man' (no longer the original man, but the *'homo absconditus'* of the future).

For faith to continue Christian in its commitment, for the resistance of history not to transform militancy into desperation, so as not to confuse historical patience—what the New Testament calls 'perseverance'—with resignation and abdication from the struggle, nor militant impatience with the inability to hope and believe in the kingdom of God without seizing hold of it, we must not forget that in the New Testament, the imperative (be converted) follows the indicative (the kingdom has been given to you), and that between the first man and the new man stands the 'second Adam', the crucified of all histories, seeking his historical fulfilment in us.

(iii) The third typology

The Christology of von Balthasar, in its way, has to face the same problems. His way of doing theology—Johannine in inspiration and tone—has the fascination of all Christology 'from above', and runs the same risk: not bearing sufficiently in mind that the God of Christians was revealed only in the historical man Jesus of Nazareth. Can one really start 'from above', from the incarnation *of God*, as though *becoming man* were accidental and secondary in his *being-God*? What then would Jesus Christ reveal?

Such marked stress on the Incarnation (from above, *a priori*, transcendental) ends by reducing Jesus' earthly life to the total passivity of a receptacle. Growth, conflict, the dramatic character of the story are as though absorbed in the all-embracing fascination of the Absolute. Contemplation of the unity ends by suppressing the road to it. It is not by chance that this Christology finds difficulty in integrating the novelty of the Word 'becoming flesh'. Because if it is true that the Word of God had to 'become used' historically to living among men (St Ireneaus), the astonishment of the man Jesus at 'becoming used' to the Word of God cannot have been any less true.

This difficulty, which applies both to method and content, since the content of faith is inseparable from the historical route by which it came about, is shown up in two themes characteristic of von Balthasar: the theology of the Cross and the kenotic interpretation of obedience. Abstracted from history, from the causes and conflicts that brought it about, as well as from the element of surprise it involved for Jesus, the Cross becomes an end in itself. But this is forgetting that the Cross, before being a theological concept, was a historical scandal. Much the same can be said of the tension between 'trinitarian obedience' and 'kenotic obedience': the first seems to pass over the struggle and conflict inherent in obedience, while the second suggests the 'break' of total abandonment. For von Balthasar, the tension is resolved in the 'Thy will be done' of the Garden of Gethsemane (*MySal*, p. 196; cf 207f; *Pul*, p. 139). But one needs to ask whether the predominance of *kenosis* (the Incarnation ordered to the Passion, almost as though it were a temporary renunciation of being God: *MySal*, pp. 143ff; *Pul*, p. 139) does not need to be balanced by other aspects. This is really going back to the old question of the 'motives' for the Incarnation, though the form it takes in von Balthasar is the classic tension between John and the Synoptics, between the school of Alexandria and that of Antioch, between modern Christology 'from above' and that 'from below'. These are dialectically complementary movements, not mutually exclusive alternatives. John comes after Mark, both theologically and in time.

The temptation is always to concentrate on the fascination of isolated elements. But the New Testament always calls us to see the complementary nature of things, to see God and man (based on Jesus Christ) not as rivals, but as freely related (God the creator) with man constituted as 'hearer', so that autonomy (anthropology) becomes obedience (to God), in order to receive our being from him as a gift. This is why it is important to examine the obedience of Jesus as a Christological concept with such strict care and attention.

Translated by Paul Burns

Notes

1. It has been necessary to select writers for the purposes of this article. This does not imply a value judgment on those chosen, even though such a process can never be entirely free from subjective elements. The criteria on which the selection was made are the following: (i) *geographic*—comparison of writers from the Germanic world with others of the (no less European) Latin world and with some representatives of the theology of Latin America; and (ii) *theological*, which is inseparable from the geographic since the theological approach of each writer cannot be separated from the socio-cultural context in which his Christianity is experienced.

2. An intriguing pointer is the relative absence, not only of the theme, but of the word itself, in analytical indexes and even in the big theological dictionaries.

3. Obeying *men*: the view that predominates from St Thomas onward, with his study of obedience in the context of justice, i.e., as a communitary virtue, a necessity for social survival. See *Summa Th.*, 2a, 2ae. Q 104f.

4. W. Pannenberg *Grundzüge der Christologie* (Gütersloh, 1964, ⁴1972), p. 30; see pp. 43f, 334, 362 and *passim*. Hereafter, pages cited in the text refer to this work.

5. This sums up a major preoccupation in the manner (and method) of theological approach in the writers chosen, though there are considerable differences between them. They are: J. I. González Faus *Acceso a Jesús: Ensayo de teología narrativa* (Salamanca ²1979) (=*Acceso*); Id. *La humanidad nueva: Ensayo de Cristología* 2 vols. (Madrid 1974) (= *Humanidad*); Ch. Duquoc *Jésus homme libre: esquisse d'une christologie* (Paris 1974) (= *Esquisse*); and in Latin America: L. Boff *Jesus Cristo libertador* (Petrópolis ²1972) (= *Jesus Cristo*); Id. *Paixão de Cristo, paixão do mundo: os fatos, as interpretações e o significado ontem e hoje* (Petrópolis 1977) (= *Paixão*); Id. *O Pai nosso: a oraçã da libertação integral* (Petrópolis 1979) (= *Pai nosso*); J. Sobrino *Cristología desde América Latina* (Mexico ²1977) (*Cristología*). Hereafter, references are given to the abbreviated title and page in the text.

6. H. U. von Balthasar *Herrlichkeit: eine theologische Ästhetik* I (= *H.* I), III/2 (= *H.* III/2) (Einsiedeln ²1961 and 1969); Id. *Theologie der Geschichte* (Einsiedeln 1959) (= *ThG*); Id *Das Ganze im Fragment* (Einsiedeln 1963) (= *GimF*); Id. 'El misterio pascual' in *Mysterium Salutis* III/2 (Madrid 1971) pp. 143-335; (= *MySal*); Id. *Pneuma und Institution* (Einsiedeln 1974) (= *PuI.*); Id. *La foi du Christ: cinq approches christologiques* (Paris 1968) (= *Foi*). Hereafter, references are given to the abbreviated title and page in the text.

Contributors

CLODOVIS BOFF, born in Brazil in 1944, is a priest of the Order of the Servants of Mary. He holds a doctorate in theology from Louvain and teaches at the Pontifical Catholic University of Rio de Janeiro. Besides numerous review articles, he has published *Teologia e Prática* (1978), *Comunidade Eclesial—Comunidade Política* (1978), *Sinais dos Tempos* (1979), and, with Leonardo Boff, *Da Libertação* (1979).

CHRISTIAN DUQUOC O.P. was born in Nantes in 1926; he was ordained in 1953. He has studied at the Dominican Study House in Leysse, France, the University of Fribourg, Switzerland, at Le Saulchoir and at the Ecole Biblique in Jerusalem. Having gained his doctorate in theology, he now teaches Dogmatics at the Faculty of Theology in Lyons, and is a member of the Editorial Board of the review *Lumière et Vie*. His published work includes *L'Église et le Progrès* and *Christologie*, 2 vols., Paris 1972.

TULLO GOFFI was born in Prevalle, Brescia, Italy, and is a doctor *utriusque iuris*. He is currently professor of moral and spiritual theology at the theological seminary in Brescia and in the Faculty of Theology of northern Italy in Milan. His principal pulbications include *Amore e sessualità* (Brescia 1964), *Obbedienze e autonomia personale*[2] (Milan 1968), *Etica sessuale cristiana*[2] (Bologna 1972), *Etica cristiana in acculturazione marxista* (Assisi 1975), *Ethos popolare* (Brescia 1979), and he has edited the *Nuovo Dizionario di spiritualità*[2] (Rome 1979).

BAS VAN IERSEL was born in 1924 in Heerlen (The Netherlands), became a Montfort father and was ordained in 1950. He studied at the universities of Nijmegen and Louvain, and obtained a doctorate in theology. At the moment he is professor of exegis of the New Testament at Nijmegen University and a member of the editorial staff of *Tijdschrift voor Theologie* and *Schrift*. Among his publications is *'Der Sohn' in den synoptischen Jesusworten* (1961).

PIERRE DE LOCHT was born in Brussels in 1916 and ordained priest in 1940. He is a doctor of theology of Louvain University. Since 1946 he has been engaged in marriage and family counselling. He was professor of moral theology in Zaïre in 1957-8. Since 1967 he has conducted seminars at Louvain and teaches at the Institute of Familial and Sexological Sciences. He has published many articles on morals, sexual ethics and marriage. Among his books are *A la mesure de son Amour* (Paris 1961) and *Les couples et l'Église* (Paris 1979).

CARLOS PALACIO S.J. was born in Spain in 1942, and has lived in Brazil since 1960. He studied at Louvain and was ordained in 1970, taking a doctorate at the Gregorian in 1975. He teaches systematic theology at the Catholic University of Rio de Janeiro. His publications include *Jesucristo: historia e interpretación* (1978), and, in collaboration with others, *Religião e catolicismo popular* (1977) and *Puebla: desafíos a la Vida Religiosa* (1979).

JEAN-CLAUDE SAGNE O.P. was born in 1936 in Tours, France, and was ordained priest in 1963. He holds degrees in literature and theology and a doctorate in the psychology of religion. He teaches social psychology at the University of Lyon-II. He has written three books on sin and repentance and is part author of *Présence du renouveau charismatique* (Paris 1979).

EDWARD SCHILLEBEECKX O.P. was born at Antwerp (Belgium) in 1914 and was ordained in 1941. He studied at Louvain, Le Saulchoir, the Ecole des Hautes Etudes and the Sorbonne (Paris). He became a doctor of theology in 1951 and magister in 1959. Since 1958, he has been teaching dogmatic theology and hermeneutics at the University of Nijmegen (Netherlands). He is the editor-in-chief of the *Tijdschrift voor Theologie*. In addition to very many articles, he has written a number of books, including *Christ the Sacrament of the Encounter with God* (New York 1963), *Revelation and Theology* (London 1968), *God and Man* (New York 1969), *World and Church* (New York 1971), *The Understanding of Faith* (London and New York 1974), *Jesus, An Experiment in Christology* (New York 1979), *Christ. The Christian Experience in the Modern World* (London and New York 1980) and many others.